THE PSYCHOLOGY AND
PSYCHOTHERAPY OF OTTO RANK

Rank in the Freudian "Inner Circle." Photograph taken about 1922.

(Sitting from left to right) Sigmund Freud, Sandor Ferenczi, Hanns Sachs; (Standing from left to right) Otto Rank, Karl Abraham, Max Eitingon, Ernest Jones.

(Reprinted by permission from Gregory Zilboorg, *A History of Medical Psychology*, W. W. Norton and Co., New York, 1941. Grateful acknowledgment is extended to Dr. Zilboorg for making the original photograph available.)

An interesting commentary on this group photograph appears in Hanns Sachs, *Freud, Master and Friend*, Chapter VIII, "The Seven Rings."

The Psychology
and Psychotherapy of
Otto Rank

An Historical and Comparative Introduction

by

FAY B. KARPF, Ph.D.

Author of

American Social Psychology: Its Origins, Development, and European Background, etc.

GREENWOOD PRESS, PUBLISHERS
WESTPORT, CONNECTICUT

The Library of Congress cataloged this book as follows:

Karpf, Fay Berger.
  The psychology and psychotherapy of Otto Rank; an
historical and comparative introduction, by Fay B. Karpf.
Westport, Conn., Greenwood Press ₁1970, ᶜ1953₁

    ix, 132 p. ports. 23 cm.

    Bibliography : p. 117–121, 131–132.

    1. Rank, Otto, 1884–1939. 2. Psychoanalysis. 3. Psychotherapy.
  I. Title.

  BF173.R36K3 1970   150.19'5   70–90539
  ISBN 0-8371-3029-8   MARC

  Library of Congress   71 ₍4₎

PREFACE

Otto Rank is today, and he has been for many years, at once one of the most controversial and influential figures in modern psychotherapy. This is not only because he was, in the words of Havelock Ellis, "perhaps the most brilliant and clairvoyant" of Freud's many pupils and associates, but also because of the significance of his many contributions to and departures from orthodox psychoanalysis. An innovator and pioneer in various areas of theory and therapy, he was a forerunner in the development of what has recently come to be known as "short-term psychotherapy" and "client-centered therapy," as well as in the early attempts to interrelate psychoanalysis and cultural anthropology, popularized at the present time in terms of the "culture-and-personality" approach to psychological and psychotherapeutic problems.

During his very active career, Rank was in close professional association not only with Freud himself for twenty years, but also with some of the most prominent American as well as European analysts, educators, and social workers. He analyzed many of the modern leaders in these fields. Through them, as well as through his own writings and teaching activities, he influenced thought and practice markedly.

His position remains today highly influential in this country, with new formulations and attempted applications by prominent adherents appearing frequently, especially through the efforts of various members of the University of Pennsylvania School of Social Work. A recent publication, *A Comparison of Diagnostic and Functional Case Work Concepts,* published by the Family Service Association of America, 1950, highlights the importance of his position in this field as the chief rival of the more orthodox Freudian position. His influence is correspondingly prominent in other fields close to analytic therapy; counseling, psychotherapy, education, guidance, various areas of group and community work and other therapy-related areas of professional endeavor.

It seems strange and almost incredible, therefore, that there should not be readily available a summary of his more important views on theory and therapy, and some account of his eventful and instructive professional career. The fact that the author of this volume was in an especially advantageous position for several years, insofar as the presentation and formulation of Rank's views are concerned, accordingly would seem to impose a responsibility, in view of his sudden and untimely death, to make more permanently available the material included in this publication.

The work was begun during Dr. Rank's lifetime and with his cooperation. It had its origin as an introduction to his own lectures given in the Graduate School for Jewish Social Work, New York City, from 1935 until his sudden death in 1939.

One part of the original material was published in *Social Work Technique* in 1937 and as a separate brochure, which was later reprinted several times, and another part was published as a separate brochure in 1940. *Social Work Technique* continued to distribute these materials for several years but recently with increasing difficulty, inasmuch as the periodical ceased publication shortly after the appearance of the second brochure. During this period also, Rank's influence was extended in several directions, in consequence of the previously mentioned Rankian-related new developments in the field of psychotherapy. These developments brought Rank's views into focus, so that there has been a more generalized and widespread interest in his position.

Accordingly, in response to repeated requests from teachers, students, and other interested persons, it was finally decided, after consultation with all concerned, to make the materials more readily available. The author consequently set about to round out and expand the presentations as seemed necessary on the basis of their previous use, until the material assumed its present form.

Since the original formulations included in Chapters V and VI had the endorsement of Dr. Rank, they have been retained, insofar as possible, in their original form. Most of the changes and additions appear in the footnotes and in the referencing. Chapter VI has also been expanded through inclusion of some illustrative material and citations from Dr. Rank's posthumously published work entitled *Beyond Psychology*. Chapters VII and VIII, as well as the "Biographical Sketch," were prepared especially for the new volume.

ACKNOWLEDGMENTS

The author wishes to acknowledge, in the first place, the courtesy of *Social Work Technique* in relinquishing its rights to the previously published parts of the material in order to facilitate the reissue of the manuscript in its new and expanded form. The author also wishes to acknowledge with gratitude various appreciative communications which have been received from instructors and others who have had occasion to use the original material. It was their continued and insistent demand for this material which provided the incentive for the present expanded publication.

Grateful acknowledgment is also made for receipt of various items of information incorporated in the "Biographical Sketch" from the following: Mrs. Beata Rank, Cambridge, Mass.; Dr. Jessie Taft, University of Pennsylvania School of Social Work; Professor Victor Kraft, University of Vienna; Professor Frederick Pollock, Institute of Social Research, Frankfort University.

Other acknowledgments are made at appropriate points in the special footnotes and references. But the writer wishes particularly to acknowledge many detailed items of information which were accumulated over the years, through direct contact with Dr. Rank himself. No formal biographical data could possibly take the place of this informally transmitted information relating to significant experiences and occurrences in his interesting career.

The author also wishes to record her indebtedness to Dr. Rank more generally for exceptional favors and constant encouragement during a professional association begun in Paris in 1934 and continued throughout the period of his residence in this country. More specific acknowledgment of his cooperation in the preparation of this material is made in the body of the text.

Acknowledgment is further made of the stimulating experience of participating in repeated class presentations by Dr. Rank and of conducting student discussions of crucial problems and questions relating to his views and to modern psychotherapy generally, especially from the standpoint of various fields of professional application.

Finally, the author desires to acknowledge her indebtedness to her husband, Dr. M. J. Karpf, for invaluable aid rendered in connection with the preparation and publication of this volume. Dating back, through the years, to common association with Dr. Rank, his own interest and experience in various fields of counseling and psychotherapy were of great value in every phase of the work, from its original conception to the present publication.

Special acknowledgment is made and thanks extended to the following publishers and authors for permission to quote from their works and, in one instance, for the reproduction of a valuable photograph:

To Alfred A. Knopf, Inc., New York, for permission to quote from O. Rank, *Art and Artist, Will Therapy* and *Truth and Reality*.

To Harcourt, Brace and Co., Inc., New York, for permission

to quote from O. Rank, *The Trauma of Birth* and A. Adler, *The Practice and Theory of Individual Psychology.*

To The Hogarth Press Ltd., London, for permission to quote from S. Freud, *Collected Papers,* Vol. I.

To W. W. Norton & Co., Inc., New York, for permission to quote from S. Freud, *New Introductory Lectures on Psychoanalysis.*

To Liveright Publishing Corp., New York, for permission to quote from S. Freud, *A General Introduction to Psychoanalysis,* Copyright 1935 by E. Bernays, renewed 1948 by S. Hoch.

To Randon House, Inc., New York, for permission to quote from A. A. Brill (trans. and ed.) *The Basic Writings of Sigmund Freud.*

To Henry Holt and Co. Inc., New York, for permission to quote from W. M. Kranefeldt, *Secret Ways of the Mind.*

To Clark University Press, Worcester, Mass., for permission to quote from Carl Murchison (ed.), *Psychologies of 1930.*

To Dr. Gregory Zilboorg, New York City, for permission to reproduce the group photograph from his *A History of Medical Psychology,* published by W. W. Norton & Co., which appears as the frontispiece of the present volume. Special thanks are extended to Dr. Zilboorg for making the original photograph available for the purpose.

To Mme. Pierre Simon, Paris, France, for permission to quote from O. Rank, *Beyond Psychology,* published privately by The Haddon Craftsmen, Inc., Camden, N. J.

To Alfred A. Knopf, Inc., New York, Robert Brunner, Psychiatric Books, New York, W. W. Norton & Co., New York, Prof. Patrick Mullahy, author of *Oedipus, Myth and Complex,* Dr. Jessie Taft, University of Pennsylvania School of Social Work, and Dr. Greta Frankly, New York City, for needed items of information and other courtesies.

F. B. K.

Beverly Hills, California, 1952.

CONTENTS

Part I
Introduction

Chapter I

"ART AND ARTIST"—A BIOGRAPHICAL
SKETCH

Otto Rank was born in Vienna in 1884, the second of two
sons in a comfortable middle-class family. His educational plans
were originally directed toward an engineering career. But these
plans were radically changed as a result of his first meeting with
Freud. Recognizing an especially gifted student along psychological lines, Freud encouraged him to consider psychology as
a career instead. Freud records the incident in interesting
fashion in his paper "On the History of the Psycho-analytic
Movement."

Freud states that from the year 1902, regular meetings of a
small group of his followers were held in his house. He describes Rank's introduction into the group as follows:

> One day a young man who had passed through the tech-
> nical training school introduced himself with a manuscript
> which showed very unusual comprehension. We induced
> him to go through the *Gymnasium* and the University and
> to devote himself to the non-medical side of psycho-analytic
> investigation. The little society acquired in him a zealous
> and dependable secretary and I gained in Otto Rank a
> faithful helper and co-worker.[1]

The manuscript to which Freud refers was the original draft
of Rank's *Der Künstler* which was published in 1907. The

---

[1] *Collected Papers,* Vol. I, p. 307.

subject-matter of this early volume represented a life-long interest of Rank's. It was, in fact, an expression of his essentially artistic temperament and thus explains the somewhat unusual title of this biographical sketch,[2] as well as some of the distinctive points of emphasis in his psychological position which center about the concept of creativity.

It so happened, also, that this deep interest of Rank's coincided with Freud's own developing interest in the cultural expansion of psychoanalysis, so that common ground and a strong bond were established between them from the first. Thus was begun a close personal and professional association between Freud and Rank which lasted for more than twenty years and which, it is pleasant to note, both men always valued highly, despite developing differences of fundamental conception and outlook during the later years of their association and despite Rank's somewhat less than pleasant relations with some others in the psychoanalytic movement, after he began to introduce innovations which were interpreted as deviating from the official psychoanalytic position.

The long-time relationship between Freud and Rank was like that of father and favored son, which both continued to view with appreciation and gratitude even though Rank, like any normal son, eventually felt that in the interest of his own further development and growth, he must regretfully emancipate himself from the too binding influence of the father figure, or rather, of the tight organizational structure to which his work gave rise. But Rank always continued to think of Freud with affection and not infrequently with suppressed longing. And Freud likewise records many appreciative statements about Rank, even after Rank began to publish the materials which eventually dissociated him from Freud's official psychoanalytic group.

Turning now to another aspect of Rank's relationship to

2 Suggested by the title of his *Art and Artist* (1932).

Freud, we find that after Rank entered the University of Vienna, he studied systematically and read widely in the fields of philosophy, psychology and history; literature and folklore; philology and culture history; art, ethics, pedagogy, and esthetics. This was in sharp contrast to Freud's own background which was narrowly medical in preoccupation, so that in this respect too Freud and Rank complemented each other. In fact, Rank proceeded in his broad cultural plan of study with Freud's approval and active sponsorship. Furthermore, Rank's cultural approach to psychological problems became the basis of their many years of collaborative association, and this type of collaboration was an important factor in eventually changing the character of psychoanalysis from a narrow medical technique to a general psychology and even a world philosophy.

A different conception of social and cultural dynamics has gradually emerged during the half century, more or less, since these early attempts to interrelate culture and psychoanalysis were initiated but, like the corresponding contemporary attempts of folk psychology, they were significant first steps in the direction of what has recently come to be known as the "culture—and—personality" approach to psychological problems. Rank had an important part to play in this wider development of psychoanalysis, first as a long-time member of the Freudian group and later, along more positive lines and new directions of thought, through the distinctive changes which he introduced into theory and therapy.

In any event, as noted, Freud had reached a point in his psychoanalytic thinking at which he was becoming increasingly interested in the extension of psychoanalytic doctrine into the social and cultural spheres. He was especially appreciative, therefore, of the broadened cultural perspective which Rank at this time introduced into psychoanalytic thinking. He records many specific statements along this line. For example, Rank called to his attention a passage in Schopenhauer in which the philosopher discusses repression. Freud makes the following comment regarding this incident:

> The doctrine of repression quite certainly came to me independently of any other source; I know of no outside impression which might have suggested it to me, and for a long time I imagined it to be entirely my own, until Otto Rank showed us the passage in Schopenhauer's *World as Will and Idea* in which the philosopher is trying to give an explanation of insanity. What he says there about the struggle against acceptance of a painful part of reality fits my conception of repression so completely that I am again indebted for having made a discovery to not being a wide reader. And yet others have read the passage and passed it by without making this discovery, and perhaps the same would have happened to me if in my young days I had had more taste for reading philosophical works. In later years I have denied myself the very great pleasure of reading the works of Nietzsche from a deliberate resolve not to be hampered in working out the impressions received in psychoanalysis by any sort of expectation derived from without. I have to be prepared, therefore—and am so, gladly—to forego all claim to priority in the many instances in which laborious psycho-analytic investigation can merely confirm the truths which this philosopher recognized intuitively.[3]

Not everybody will agree with Freud about the virtue of his isolation from related thought, but this was a characteristic of the early psychoanalytic movement and this lengthy passage is cited first, to indicate Rank's role in changing its narrow perspective and second, to illustrate the tolerance and readiness with which Freud accepted Rank's services in this respect. It might also be suggested that in this regard, Freud could well serve as a model to some of his especially ardent followers, who seem to think that in order to demonstrate their complete psychoanalytic loyalty, they must maintain, or pretend, that apart from the immediate psychoanalytic group itself, no sig-

[3] *Collected Papers*, Vol. I, p. 297.

nificant contribution is ever made in the field of psychotherapy.[4]

In the course of the more than twenty years of his close association with Freud, Rank, under Freud's sponsorship, understandably achieved prestige, influence, and a favored position in the psychoanalytic movement. In addition to a series of brilliant publications dealing with the wider aspects of psychoanalysis in the fields of literature, art, and mythology, he continued as secretary of the Vienna psychoanalytic group; in collaboration with Hanns Sachs, he established and edited the journal *Imago* (1912-24);[5] he also edited the *Internationale Zeitschrift für Psychoanalyse* (1919-24); likewise, he founded and became the director of the International Psychoanalytic Institute of Vienna (1919-24); and in collaboration with Ferenczi, he prepared a valued monograph on the technical aspects of psychoanalysis (Eng. trans., *The Development of Psychoanalysis*, 1925), to say nothing of many other services and minor publications.

[4] A classic example is a statement by A. A. Brill in his "Introduction" to *The Basic Writings of Sigmund Freud* (1938). After tracing out the high-points of Freud's history of the psychoanalytic movement, Brill says: "I could continue and give an elaborate description of Freud's works and struggles since the publication of his history of the psychoanalytic movement in 1914. Basically, nothing of importance has happened within the movement besides the defection of Otto Rank, who, like Adler and Jung, left Professor Freud after having devoted many years of valuable work to psychoanalysis. Reflecting on the works of the Freudian secessionists, I feel that none of them has contributed anything of real value to mental science since they separated themselves from the master. All of them, however, have made contributions of a special kind to the literature of psychology. . . . . His disciples, of whom there are many the world over, have made impressive contributions to the mental sciences, but a deep study of these productions will show nothing that is so novel as not to have been anticipated or implied by the master himself." (*The Basic Writings of Sigmund Freud*, p. 31.)

In line with this viewpoint, such a recognized interpreter of Freud as O. Fenichel, in his *The Psychoanalytic Theory of Neurosis* (*1945*), cites Rank's works only up to the time he published his controversial *Trauma of Birth* (1924). Thereafter, presumably, Rank's works, which until then had always been so highly valued, had at once become psychoanalytically irrelevant.

[5] The theory underlying the establishment of this journal was formulated by Rank and Sachs in *The Significance of Psychoanalysis for the Mental Sciences* (Eng. trans., 1916).

It would thus appear that Rank had attained a satisfying and even enviable position in the psychoanalytic movement. And yet toward the end of this period, he was getting increasingly restless. Psychoanalysis, through the years and as the psychoanalytic movement gained popularity and momentum, was hardening into a standardized procedure. Instead of the inventive and creative adventure it had been in the early years, it was increasingly taking form as a routine technique. All this ran counter to Rank's artistic temperament and his developing view of the central importance of creative flexibility in the therapeutic process. He began to chafe under the tightening restrictions of the accepted pattern of psychoanalytic thought and practice. Inevitably, he accordingly began to seek out lines of experimentation and innovation which, for the time being, he continued to view in the same light as all his previous contributions, insights to be shared with his associates and incorporated into the general body of psychoanalytic doctrine.

Along about 1922, however, he also began to elaborate on the theoretical meaning and significance of his innovations, still in the same spirit of collaboration as heretofore and with no thought of revolutionary deviation. Even in his *Trauma of Birth,* which documents some of his deviant views, he entertained no thought of separation from the psychoanalytic group. In fact, he dedicated the volume to Freud and certainly meant to do him honor by this means.

The unexpected storm of controversy which the publication of this volume precipitated, therefore took Rank by surprise and also left him, for a time, greatly distressed. However, he confidently expected that the storm would presently die down and, perhaps, he also expected Freud to take a stand in his favor. But as the situation developed, it got to be even beyond Freud's control. He had no choice but to support those who were seemingly defending his position. To ease matters all around, Rank decided to leave Vienna for Paris, there to await further developments. Since the situation failed to improve, it finally turned out that this act of physical separation likewise marked his actual severance from the Vienna group.

Everything considered, Rank was left with the regretful feeling that the rift between him and Freud was forced on them, against the wishes of both. No doubt professional jealousy was a factor in the situation, for Rank was often referred to, after Jung and Adler, as the most brilliant of the group and this, seemingly, was a challenge to some of the other members of the group. Some of them were also envious of Rank's influential position in the psychoanalytic movement and seized at the opportunity to undermine him in the eyes of his associates. But most of all, the view was prominent that Rank had set out to follow in the footsteps of Jung and Adler and that, like them, he had opened the group to unfavorable outside criticism, a disloyalty which the sectarian mentality, fostered by the much criticized and over-defensive psychoanalytic movement, could not forgive.

We have a demonstration of this same intolerant over-defensiveness again at the present time in the reactions of the official psychoanalytic group to such reinterpretations as are represented, for example, by the work of some of the neo-Freudians, especially the critical work of Karen Horney. One scarcely dares to mention her name in the presence of some of the official defenders of the orthodox psychoanalytic position. The history of the psychoanalytic movement is unfortunately punctuated by a long series of such manifestations of intolerance to innovation, in consequence of which the orthodox psychoanalytic group has lost some of its most original and creative members, to the serious impoverishment of its own ranks and the unprofitable division of the field as a whole.

But it is again pleasant to note that Freud himself did not at this time or any other time, become vindictive as did some of his followers in his name. On the contrary, he continued to refer to Rank, as always, appreciatively. For example, eight

years (1932) after the publication of Rank's *Trauma of Birth,*
Freud wrote as follows:

> Otto Rank, to whom psycho-analysis owes many valuable
> contributions, has also the merit of having strongly em-
> phasized the importance of the act of birth and of separa-
> tion from the mother. It is true that the rest of us found it
> impossible to accept the extreme deductions that he drew
> from this factor with regard to the theory of the neuroses
> and even to analytical therapy. But before this he had
> already discovered the central feature of his doctrine,
> namely, that the anxiety-experience of birth is the proto-
> type of all later danger-situations.[6]

In fact, Freud regarded this "central feature" of Rank's doctrine
of sufficient significance to make it basic in his revised theory
of anxiety.[7] And yet, it was precisely this theory of Rank's, as
developed in his *Trauma of Birth,* which precipitated so much
defensive controversy in the movement that it eventually
forced an unwilling break between Freud and Rank.

It thus came about, that after so many years of devoted service in the interest of the psychoanalytic movement, Rank finally
realized that with his departure for Paris in 1926, he had actually dissociated himself from the official psychoanalytic group
and that he was now completely free to formulate his deviant

[6] *New Introductory Lectures on Psychoanalysis,* p. 122.

[7] *New Introductory Lectures on Psychoanalysis,* p. 119 ff.; *The Problem of
Anxiety,* p. 99 ff.

An intimate account of Rank's close association with Freud and his important
role in the psychoanalytic movement until he published his *Trauma of Birth,*
appears in Hanns Sachs, *Freud: Master and Friend,* especially pp. 15, 49, 62, 120,
149, 160.

Sachs states: "For many years Rank had been Freud's trusted assistant, collabo-
rator, disciple, and friend, bound to him by the strongest ties of allegiance,
gratitude, and communion of thought. Freud appreciated highly his restless
energy and sharp intelligence; he had done everything in his power to make
Rank's way through life smooth and to bestow on him a leading part in the psychoanalytic movement." As regards *The Trauma of Birth,* Sachs reports: "Freud
tried for a while to mediate, but with little success since the gulf between
Rank's new opinions and the psychoanalytic theory became more and more evident." pp. 149, 160.

Rank about the time of his separation
from the Vienna group, following his publication of *The Trauma of Birth* (1924).

views. This he set about to do in earnest. It was understandably a difficult, painful, and piece-meal process of realization, but it had its substantial compensations. For it eventually set him free from the restraints of psychoanalytic interpretation, so that he could work unhampered toward the independence of thought and outlook, toward which he had for years been struggling against heavy odds and increasingly trying conditions.

He was still to learn that, difficult as was his physical separation from his associates, his intellectual emancipation from the twenty year hold of his association with the psychoanalytic group, was a still more difficult feat of achievement. For example, he set about courageously to formulate his views (more or less systematically, or as systematically as he ever attempted the task) in his projected *Technik der Psychoanalyse* (1926, 1929, 1931) in three parts or volumes. But by the time the second volume was completed, he realized that certain theoretical discrepancies were in evidence, due to the fact that in the first volume he still essentially followed the psychoanalytic pattern of thought, whereas in the second volume and likewise in the third, he had passed on increasingly to the presentation of his own distinctive views. This gradual change of emphasis accounts for the troubling inconsistencies in his writings of the period and, in consequence, for the varied interpretations of his essential position which are sometimes gleaned from his works.

In view of his observed theoretical discrepancies, Rank tried to change the title of the second two volumes, in order to make clear his shift of position. But the publisher would not make the change in mid-publication. Rank did the next best thing, namely, he gave special emphasis to the central concepts of his developing position, concepts which have since become identified with his later works, as the following historical introduction will outline in some detail. But he never again used the designation "psychoanalysis" in the titles of his works and even elsewhere, he tried to substitute the broader term "psychotherapy" whenever possible. Rank thus gradually emerged from the narrow confines of the isolated psychoanalytic group and entered into the wider sphere of more general thought about psychology and psychotherapy.

An important result of this change of emphasis has been the spread of Rank's influence in new directions, a process which has been facilitated by his continued efforts to set forth his developing position in a series of additional publications, as will be noted in the following discussion of his views. Rank's expanding influence has furthermore been advanced by the tendency which the orthodox psychoanalytic group has shown in recent years and especially in this country, to narrow its interest again chiefly to the field of medical practice. Related professional groups are accordingly perforce beginning to look elsewhere for the assistance which, for a time, they sought almost exclusively from psychoanalysis: general psychiatry, clinical psychology, group dynamics, education, the social and cultural sciences, as well as psychotherapy in the broader views of Rank and others.

Under these circumstances, it is natural that independent therapeutic groups should be developing, such for example as the increasingly popular Rogerian group. It is instructive to note how this group and other similar recent developments in this country seek to relate themselves to Rank's work. Apart from interest in the distinctive technical features characteristic of Rank's position, it is his general viewpoint as a whole which appeals and appears to fit into the traditional pattern of American culture more consistently than the Freudian system in its wider implications. Especially significant in this connection has been Rank's positive, constructive, self-determining and self-directing orientation, in contrast to the Freudian negative, reductive, and closely-knit authoritarian viewpoint.

For, being so definitely biological in orientation, Freud had an extremely serious blind-spot insofar as the social and cultural aspects of human life are concerned. He always viewed social life only in terms of its curbs, prohibitions, and limitations, never in terms of its positive social and cultural values, as the necessary instrumentalities for the fulfillment of human life. Furthermore, Freud's viewpoint is limited by what has come to be termed "the pathological fallacy" as a result of which, he viewed the entire world through the colored glasses of the abnormal.[8] He never thought to check his observations and conclusions on the normal population of his own culture, to say nothing about the limitations of his generalizations, insofar as other cultures are concerned. He simply assumed the processes he was observing were universal, as was the custom at the time, during the earlier especially productive period of his psychoanalytic findings.

The serious effect of these limitations in the Freudian system of thought, has been to undermine man in the dignity of his *human* heritage and functioning, and constantly to pull him down to the level of animal and pathological behavior. This, rather than any specific theory, except as such theory is an expression of the above-noted leveling-down procedure, has been the real basis of opposition to Freud's system (in contrast to his specific clinical contributions) and the significant occasion for the resulting important series of deviant positions which have marked the history of psychoanalysis, beginning with Jung, Adler, and Rank and continuing to the present in the works of some of the neo-Freudian group.

Rank likewise began with these limitations, but his viewpoint was gradually balanced, first by his interest in the artist type as over against the neurotic type, and second by his wide acquaintance with general thought and culture. Then, these corrective leanings were confirmed and strengthened by his first-hand personal contact with three national cultures, as he shifted his place of residence from Vienna, to Paris, to New York City. These special experiences served, in his case, as a corrective of the one-sidedness of Freud's viewpoint and gradually led him

8 Rank, *Beyond Psychology*, p. 288.

in the distinctive directions characteristic of his later position.

After Rank established himself in Paris, he divided his time for several years between France and the United States until 1935, when he settled permanently in New York City. For some time, he had been concentrating on the analysis of American patients and his experience with them impressed upon him differences between them and his European patients which, he felt, were an expression of the more democratic character of their family organization and relationships. This insight which was later strengthened by intimate contact with American colleagues, students, and social agencies made him feel the kinship of his views with American thought about culture and personality and led him gradually to a fuller recognition of the importance of the social and cultural factor in the determination of personality and human behavior. He thus developed an outlook, in many respects characteristic of the more positive aspects of the recent social-psychological approaches to human problems.

Only his sudden and early death in 1939, when Rank was still at the height of his productivity, probably prevented him from giving more adequate theoretical expression to this newly confirmed but deeply personal and congenial viewpoint. This was a great loss to psychotherapy as well as to more general thought, for at the time of his death, Rank was actually engaged in consolidating his thinking along these lines, through a renewed interest in the psychology of learning, the self, growth and change, personality and government. The germs of his partially formulated viewpoint are, however, clearly in evidence in several of his later works, including his posthumously published volume entitled *Beyond Psychology* (1941), where he relates his position to a "psychology of difference" in terms of culture and social change.

These important considerations help to explain Rank's expanding influence in this country despite seemingly insuperable obstacles. Without any organization to perpetuate and disseminate his views; without any of the official paraphernalia identified with the interpretation of psychoanalytic doctrine; without even an easily available systematic presentation of his thought, or the easy conversational style of Freud's writings; without any of these aids and with the further handicap of writing in a difficult Germanic style—Rank's influence has nevertheless established itself to the point where, in some fields, it is practically the only rival of the accepted pattern of currently interpreted Freudian thought. This, for example, is the situation in the psychoanalytically dominated field of social work.

This has come about single-handedly, one might say, and in a very few years, through Rank's own efforts and a small creative following, which has steadily refused to be intimidated by the claims of special authoritativeness on the part of the official psychoanalytic group. In this line-up, Rank's position has been and continues to be a wholesome and liberating influence. Retaining so much of the content and general direction of psychoanalytic thought, and yet remaining so flexibly and creatively adaptable to new insights and developments, Rank's position has been a stimulus and an incentive toward further experimentation and innovation in the currently controversial field of psychotherapy. His very inconstancies and difficulty of style, though certainly no advantage generally, have in this particular connection, proved to be a source of advance. For one cannot, in his case, as in Freud's, adopt an esoteric and over-simplified terminology to be used in standardized fashion. One must ponder his writings and meanings and selectively incorporate them into one's own thinking and experience. This, in itself, has been a factor making for a more flexible and creative utilization of his views, by contrast to the highly stylized pattern of psychoanalytic doctrine, as was Rank's intention and as he continued to stress in all his later works. It naturally also produced inconsistencies of interpretation, as must be evident from the varied developments which link themselves, directly or indirectly, to Rank's views, among them "short" therapy, "client-centered" therapy, "non-directive" therapy, relationship-oriented education and group discussion, service-oriented or functional counseling and case work, and others.

Dr. Jessie Taft, the translator of Rank's later works and an outstanding interpreter of his position in the field of social work, states:

> If one were to pick out the particular attitude which finally led Rank to a new comprehension of the therapeutic task on which he had worked in association with Freud for so many years, one might well select his complete respect for the personality of the neurotic patient, combined with the absence of medical presupposition which freed him from the tendency to regard the neurosis as illness.[9]

The two parts of this characterization are interlinked and together they define the non-authoritarian atmosphere of Rank's therapeutic approach and general thought.

This was not always the direction of Rank's emphasis. During his Freudian period, he was as ideologically authoritarian as any other orthodox Freudian. It was during his post-Freudian period that he gradually arrived at his distinctive non-authoritarian position as reflected in his insistence on "the equal right of every individual to become and be himself, which actually means to accept his own difference and have it accepted by others."[10] Insofar as therapy is concerned, this means that the patient has rights as a self-responsible person to determine his own destiny, a view which the Freudian therapist-oriented concept of "resistance" contradicts, according to Rank.

It is particularly instructive to follow out the process of Rank's dissociation from the official psychoanalytic movement because he tried so long and so hard to remain a part of it. Eventually, he found this to be impossible on the terms demanded; his intellectual honesty and personal integrity would

9 Rank, *Will Therapy*, p. xi.
10 *Beyond Psychology*, p. 267.

not permit it. It is hardly surprising, in view of Rank's history and direction of development, that his position should appeal to those who, for one reason or another, likewise become dissatisfied with the Freudian system of thought, especially since the alternatives in the field of psychotherapy are still so limited. In some situations, it practically becomes a choice between Freud and Rank, between psychotherapy narrowly conceived as a medical problem or broadly conceived as a human problem, in the broad sense of development, education, and adjustment.

So it is that, despite all opposition and criticism, Rank's influence persists and continues to appeal to American practitioners in various areas of therapeutic endeavor. It is of some importance, therefore, to sketch out the development of his deviant views. This is the purpose of the following historical introduction and outline of the essentials of his distinctive position.

Part II

Analytic Background

Chapter II

THE FREUDIAN BACKGROUND—
PSYCHOANALYSIS[1]

The term, "psychoanalysis," is commonly used to refer to the entire analytic field, but in the technical literature of the analytic schools themselves, it has been restricted to the system of Sigmund Freud as distinguished from the divergent schools which have, in the course of time, separated from it. The practice has thus grown up of referring to Freud's system as "psychoanalysis" in contradistinction to the other well-known formulations of analytic doctrine, such as C.G., Jung's "analytical psychology," Alfred Adler's "individual psychology," and what is here termed descriptively, Otto Rank's "will" or "dynamic relationship" psychology. These distinctive characterizations are in themselves interesting and suggestive, for it is possible to get some insight into these different formulations and their respective lines of emphasis merely from a consideration of the above designations.

It is necessary to note before proceeding, however, since the point is so frequently overlooked, that psychoanalysis, even if taken in the restricted sense, has a considerable history preceding Freud. It is illuminating for our purposes to view the move-

[1] This outline relating to Freudian, Jungian, and Adlerian theory and therapy is presented as necessary background for the appreciation of Rank's deviant position and not as a comprehensive analysis or descriptive summary of the systems themselves. The writer wishes to acknowledge particularly Dr. Rank's cooperation in the original preparation of the material, especially in the presentation of his own position in relation to these systems.

ment in its larger historical setting, for one thus gets a sense of chronology and relationship which is helpful in appraising certain aspects of the situation that are otherwise much more difficult to comprehend. It is valuable to bear in mind, for example, that Freud's own background connects up directly with the Paris and Nancy schools of psychiatry and their respective viewpoints regarding hypnosis and its use in the treatment of hysteria. For the distrust with which psychoanalysis has always been met in some circles, especially in the earlier period of its development, has in part been an inheritance from this association and the earlier movements of mesmerism and the like which this association calls to mind. Even present-day attitudes are colored by this association and certain aspects of early procedure which followed from it. Analytic therapy, it must be admitted, is still regarded by the critical as a cult which draws upon the suggestible and credulous elements of the population.[2]

Less directly, perhaps, insofar as his technique is concerned but quite as vitally insofar as his theoretical position is concerned, Freud's background also links up intimately with certain general tendencies of thought of the day, for example, the anti-intellectualism, evolutionism, and atomistic materialism which were so widely characteristic of nineteenth century thought. In the field of psychology, these tendencies resulted in a biologically reductive viewpoint in respect to which important movements of reaction have since developed, such as behavioristic, Gestalt, and social psychology in their wider implications. These connections are mentioned because such perspective encourages an open-mindedness which is essential in the field of analysis and is especially necessary if one is to appreciate the divisions which have, in the past several decades, developed within its own field of endeavor.

[2] For example, Milton Harrington, *Wish-hunting in the Unconscious, An Analysis of Psychoanalysis* (1934) ; Emil Ludwig, *Doctor Freud, An Analysis and a Warning* (1947) ; Andrew Salter, *The Case Against Psychoanalysis* (1951).

With this bare suggestion of general background, we pass on to a brief consideration of the formulations themselves, necessarily in highly schematized form. On this account, it will be necessary to assume at this point, some background knowledge of the subject which can come into play to fill in details of content that cannot be touched upon in this brief outline. This is especially important in respect to Freudian doctrine, for its strength has consisted peculiarly in concrete content rather than in generalized formulation. Moreover, some familiarity with the distinctive content of Freudian thought must be assumed throughout in this discussion, otherwise a brief consideration of specific lines of deviation from the Freudian position would be unintelligible.

Freudian doctrine should, in fact, be studied developmentally, for it has passed through a series of elaborations, restatements, and alterations the significance of which is otherwise lost. But if we take a cross-section view of Freud's system in more or less completed form, it may be said to rest chiefly on the following basic concepts: (1) the foundational concept of "the unconscious" and the associated concept of "repression," (2) the explanatory concept of "psychosexuality," especially "infantile sexuality," and the interrelated concept of "sublimation," (3) the treatment concepts of "resistance" and "transference," along with the special devices of "free association," "dream analysis," and insight "interpretation," and also (4) the concepts connected with Freud's later reformulations of his theory in terms of "id," "ego," and "super-ego" and finally, in terms of "eros" and the "death instinct."

Some Freudians, with some encouragement from Freud himself, refer to the earlier aspects of his doctrine as dealing directly with psychoanalytic observation or fact in contrast to his later more generalized reformulations which Freud himself in part characterized as speculative theory.[3] But it is clear to any im-

3 Ives Hendrick, *Facts and Theories of Psychoanalysis* (1934, 1939), for example, is organized from this standpoint.

partial student that such a distinction is merely relative and that, in reality, no part of Freud's system is altogether free from theory, since his basic terminology introduces theory of a most controversial nature. In fact, so important a part is theory in Freud's facts of observation that it is actually necessary to understand his whole system in order to get at their special meaning. The same may, of course, be said of any system, for the characteristic of a system is that the part takes on meaning in terms of the whole. It is especially important to note this in the case of Freud, however, not only because of the special meanings which he attaches to his terms but also because the claim is made for his doctrine that it is not merely a theoretical system but also a scientific structure.

Let us take the fundamental concepts of "the unconscious" and "repression" by way of illustration. That the whole content of mental life is not subject to recall at any one time may be a fact, but whether this is because part of it is "unconscious" in the Freudian sense or represents "the unconscious" and so is pathologically inaccessible to recall is, of course, altogether a matter of theory. Again, it may be a fact that there is special difficulty in recalling certain aspects of personal experience, but whether this justifies the Freudian doctrine of "repression" is another matter and a very controversial point of theory. In the same way, the theoretical components of the other crucial concepts of the Freudian system may be brought out, as will appear strikingly in some of the departures from the Freudian position which we shall consider.

Nevertheless, as already suggested, the strong point of psychoanalytic doctrine, especially during the earlier period, has been its closeness to experiential or empirical fact. It is interesting to note how some of these facts were used by Freud in the formulation of his doctrine. He found from his early contact with the field and especially from observation of Charcot's work that hysterical symptoms could be produced and dispelled by hypnotic suggestion. He thus concluded that ideas were somehow the effective factors in the situation. Working with Breuer, he also found that under hypnosis hysterical patients could be made to recall crucial experiences connected with their symptoms which, it seemed, they could not recall in the normal state; and furthermore, that the recall of such experiences apparently resulted in the disappearance of the hysterical symptoms, especially if the recollection was accompanied by a vivid reproduction of the original emotion associated with the experiences. This was therapy by the so-called method of hypnotic abreaction or psychotharsis. From it, Freud drew further highly important conclusions, for example, that the ideas which were pathologically effective in hysteria were connected with psychically traumatic events in the lives of the patients, that they apparently operated in dissociation from normal consciousness, and that they were associated with a high level of emotional tension which mirrored the emotional tone originally attaching to the experiences themselves.

Basing his position on such observations and conclusions and supported by certain theories of hypnotic suggestion and personality dissociation which were current at the time, Freud in collaboration with Breuer, formulated the so-called "traumatic" theory of hysteria, in which the concepts of repression and the unconscious appear for the first time in preliminary form. Certain psychically traumatic experiences, because they are too painful to bear, are excluded or "repressed" from consciousness. They then lead an independent and dissociated existence apart from consciousness, while the emotional tension associated with the experiences persists and remains active. Since this emotional tension does not have a normal outlet in consciousness, it seeks abnormal expression in the form of hysterical symptoms. If, however, the traumatic experiences can be brought back into consciousness under appropriate conditions, the normal form of expression is restored to them and hence they lose their pathological effect.

Since these experiences could be recalled under proper conditions, it seemed logical to assume that they were preserved somewhere and this somewhere Freud called, by contrast to consciousness, "the unconscious." It is clear, however, that "the unconscious," the foundational concept of psychoanalysis, is not a matter of observation, in fact, cannot, in the nature of the case, be a matter of observation. It is an interpretive or inferential concept based on observation, with all the possibilities of error that may, as we know from the history of thought, creep into such a process. The same may be said of the concept of "repression." Repression similarly cannot be observed. It, too, is an inferential concept which Freud found indispensable in the formulation of his doctrine of the unconscious. He arrived at the concept by observation of the supposed effects of repression in the form of the obtrusive phenomenon of "resistance" in the analytic situation.[4]

Freud found later that this early method of therapy had many technical disadvantages, and also, that it was in many cases quite temporary. The treatment was symptomatic, he concluded, not basic, since it dealt only with the end result of a pathological process. While still using hypnosis, Freud discovered that many experiences which he originally thought were only accessible through hypnosis, could be recalled by patients in the normal state under proper conditions of relaxation and sympathetic encouragement. This discovery gradually led to the development of his new free association method, which has remained the cornerstone of psychoanalytic technique ever

[4] It should be noted in this connection that Freud himself termed the doctrine of repression, which he characterized as "the foundation-stone on which the whole structure of psychoanalysis rests," a theoretical formulation and in this respect, he distinguished it, along with the doctrines of sexuality and the unconscious, from the "two observed facts" of psychoanalysis: the facts of transference and of resistance. (*Collected Papers*, vol. I, pp. 298, 338). However, the above considerations apply also to these "observed facts" as interpreted by Freud, and hence, differentiation of fact and theory in psychoanalytic doctrine becomes a hazardous undertaking. Other writers have, therefore, not in general observed this distinction as made by Freud, especially since Freud was himself not consistent in holding to it.

since. By free association, Freud could push beyond the adult traumata revealed in hypnosis to earlier experiences, until he reached the limits of recall in infancy. By this means, too, he seemed to be able to establish the relationship of sexual experiences and impulses to neurotic symptoms, a theory which had been maturing in his mind from his first contact with hysterical patients. He thus arrived at his concept of "psychosexuality" and his emphasis on "infantile sexuality," which involved a radical change of technique, based now, on a detailed review of the patient's whole life history with special emphasis on the infantile period.

But here again, we see that the Freudian concept of psychosexuality and especially of infantile sexuality is not an observation merely but an interpretation and in this case, furthermore, the interpretation is definitely an outgrowth of the free association technique. If we push association further and further back, we must eventually come to infantile experiences. This does not establish infantile experiences as primary in an etiological but only in an historical sense. Moreover, the fact that association stops with the infantile period does not establish this period as the origin of the pathological process; it may be only a limitation of the free association method, unless, of course, we are willing in the first place to accept Freud's doctrine of the unconscious and repression as basic in mental disorder. The more general doctrine of psychosexuality does not suffer from this disadvantage so conspicuously, but less directly it is open to similar uncertainties. In any event, criticism of Freudian doctrine has always concentrated on his concept of psychosexuality and its elaboration in psychoanalytic theory.

All sorts of explanations have been advanced to account for the appearance of sexual material in the psychoanalytic process, other than the one which Freud adopted. For example, it has been claimed, that the neurotic is preoccupied with the subject not because it is etiological in his disorder but because of his conflicts and failures in other spheres. Also, it has been maintained that the psychoanalytic process, in the nature of the situation, places a premium on the production of this type of material, precisely because of the importance which the Freudian analyst attaches to it. This view is strengthened by the observation that analyses differ strikingly in this respect, in accordance with the standpoint from which they are carried on. Non-Freudian analyses apparently do not elicit so much sexual material, but' on the other hand, they elicit other types of material, which reflect the particular standpoint of the analyst. These considerations have, for the most part, come from other therapists and are based on the same kind of evidence as Freud's, so that the Freudian doctrine of psychosexuality has basically come into question.

Two brief quotations will be cited from a statement by Jung in this connection by way of illustration. He says:

It is a somewhat curious and remarkable fact in the history of science—although it pertains to the peculiar character of the psychoanalytical movement—that Freud, the creator of psychoanalysis (in the narrower sense), insists upon identifying the analytical method with his sexual theory, and thus has placed upon it the stamp of dogmatism. The "scientific" infallibility of this explanation caused me, in due time, to break with Freud, for dogma and science are to me incommensurable quantities which mutually interfere with one another through their confusion. Dogma as a factor in religion has inestimable value just because of its absolute standpoint. But when science thinks that it can do without criticism and skepticism, it degenerates into a sickly hot-house plant. One of the elements of life necessary to science is extreme uncertainty. Wherever science is inclined to dogmatize, and thus to be impatient and fanatical, it is very likely that a justifiable doubt is concealed and that an uncertainty, which is only too well founded, has been explained away . . .

No one who is interested in "psychoanalysis," and who therefore wishes to make a somewhat adequate survey of the whole field of modern medical knowledge of the soul, should fail to study the Adlerian writings. He will find them extremely stimulating, and will then for the first time make the very important discovery that exactly the same cases of neuroses can be explained in an equally convincing way from the standpoint of Freud or of Adler, despite the fact that the two methods of explanation seem to be diametrically opposed to one another.[5]

These expressed views by Freud's eminent early associate, clearly indicate the possibility of accepting the essential facts of psychosexuality, on which Freud based his position, without the particular type of emphasis which his doctrine gives them. In other words, the Freudian concept of psychosexuality is again an interpretation, and an interpretation of such challenging scope, that it runs through all of Freudian doctrine and hence, it became from the first, as we shall see, the chief battle ground of analytic controversy.[6]

The possibilities of such illustrative elaboration of the questionable aspects of psychoanalytic doctrine are limitless, but the above are sufficient to indicate the basic ground for difference of viewpoint and interpretation, not only in respect to specific psychoanalytic theories but also in respect to accepted psychoanalytic facts. We are now, accordingly, in a better position to appreciate the significance of the divergent positions which are to be considered next, and especially, the points of controversy about which they have in the first place chiefly developed.

Before passing on it is, however, necessary to add one point of general comment. This introductory analysis of Freudian

[5] W. M. Kranefeldt, *Secret Ways of the Mind*, "Introduction," pp. xxv-xxvi, xxxii-xxxiii.

[6] The concepts of repression, the unconscious, and psychosexuality were chosen for detailed consideration here because they are so widely known and so crucial in Freudian thought, but, as has already been suggested, any other concepts might have been used for the purpose, including the less generally understood concepts of resistance and transference. That other analysts do not accept the Freudian implications of resistance and transference is sufficient to indicate that there is an interpretive element in these concepts, just as in the others.

doctrine has necessarily been critical, in order to provide a background for the reinterpretations of the Freudian position which come into view in connection with the positions of Jung, Adler, and Rank. As the pioneer formulation in the field, it was inevitable that later effort should build upon Freud's work and depart from it. In this sense, all of the later formulations have, in the first place, been built up chiefly as a criticism of Freud's position. But we should not on that account overlook the more positive contributions of Freudian doctrine, which are implied throughout and are given indirect emphasis again and again, in that Freudian doctrine remains basic or, at least, is made the starting point in each of the following formulations. It is necessary to bear this in mind in order to maintain a balanced outlook on the deviant formulations which follow.

Chapter III

THE JUNGIAN BACKGROUND—ANALYTICAL PSYCHOLOGY

From about 1900, when Freud began to attract students and co-workers, for a decade or so, the psychoanalytic movement was marked by comparative harmony. Psychoanalysis was dominated by the dramatic figure of its founder and differences of viewpoint and emphasis remained submerged by the common endeavor to establish the movement. About 1910, however, these differences began to assert themselves and one after the other of Freud's more independent associates began to break away. Freudian thought had, from the first, been violently rejected by most representatives of the fields of medicine and psychology and now open conflict was being precipitated also within the ranks of the psychoanalytic group itself. Among the most important of the divergent viewpoints which were taking form at this time, were those of C. G. Jung and Alfred Adler.

Freud stated later that both of them had dissociated themselves from psychoanalysis because of their antagonistic position regarding the subject of sexuality in psychoanalytic doctrine.[1]

[1] Freud's statement on this point is of interest. He says: "Any line of investigation, no matter what its direction, which recognizes these two facts [the facts of transference and of resistance] and takes them as the starting-point of its work

31

But each of them reached this antagonistic position in characteristic manner and it is important, both for an understanding of Freudian as well as of Adlerian and Jungian doctrine, to note the actual grounds of their departure.

Jung started on the path of psychoanalysis independently and before he came under Freud's direct influence. He had done distinguished work in the field of diagnostic word association and it was through this work that he was drawn into close co-operation with Freud. Unlike Freud's other associates also, Jung was connected with an independent school from the beginning and co-operated with Freud only indirectly and through interest in common problems. As time went on, however, Jung's viewpoint diverged more and more from Freud's and he finally came to an open break with Freud in 1913 over the Freudian doctrine of libido. Jung came to feel, in particular, that Freud's extreme emphasis on sexuality was unwarranted and he concentrated this difference of viewpoint in an attempt to reinterpret the Freudian concept of libido in broader terms. "My scientific conscience," says Jung, "would not allow me to subscribe to an almost fanatical doctrine, based upon a one-sided and, therefore, false interpretation of the facts."[2]

Libido, according to Jung, is all-embracing and undifferentiated psychic energy, which can direct itself into manifold channels of human interest and activity. It is desire, longing, urge in general, corresponding to Bergson's *elan vital,* the source of all drives and affects, sexual as well as non-sexual. In fact, he recognized an elementary tendency, spiritual in character, which he regarded as anti-sexual in effect, in that it

---

may call itself psychoanalysis, though it arrives at results other than my own. But anyone who takes up other sides of the problem while avoiding these two premises will hardly escape the charge of misappropriating by attempted impersonation, if he persists in calling himself a psychoanalyst." (*Collected Papers,* vol. I, p. 298). Since neither Jung nor Adler could accept the sexual implications of these two basic psychoanalytic concepts, they have, by mutual consent, dissociated themselves from this particularistic designation.

2 *Contributions to Analytical Psychology,* p. 19.

opposes itself to primitive sexuality and ultimately transforms it into a creative principle on the psychic and cultural plane, as, for example, in the universal moral and religious strivings of mankind. The special emphasis placed by Freud on sexuality thus appeared to him to be exaggerated and one-sided and, eventually, he came to criticize the whole Freudian doctrine of psychosexuality as an unjustifiable extension of the legitimate meaning of the term sexuality, and especially as an unwarranted projection back upon the infantile period of the adult differentiated viewpoint, more particularly of the adult pathological viewpoint.

In conjunction with his libido theory, Jung also sought to broaden the Freudian concept of the unconscious. The latter, according to him, is not merely the repository of repressed personal experiences, as Freud maintained, but also of other personal experiences, and especially, it is the storehouse of the rich deposit of ancestral experiences. Jung thus came to emphasize what he has termed the "collective unconscious," alongside of the Freudian personal or individual unconscious and, in connection with it, the so-called "archetypes" or "primordial images" which, according to him, represent the collective unconscious psychologically. In seeking insight into this important part of the unconscious and the symbolism in terms of which it expresses itself, for example, in dream and phantasy, Jung was led to the study of culture materials—especially mythology, archaeology, and comparative religion. He thereby greatly extended the content and scope of analytical material and deepened it tremendously on the cultural side. Freudian doctrine deals primarily with personal history; Jung's deals also with the whole range of racial evolution and cultural development. It is phylogenetic as well as ontogenetic in reference and it is especially rich in the former direction. This difference of orientation is basic to Jung's position and sets his theory off dramatically from Freud's.

Jung used his new orientation to develop an aspect of his

theory which has become widely popular, namely, his classification of personality types in terms of extroversion and introversion. The first objective of this classification was an attempt to reconcile the conflicting positions of Freud and Adler, but later Jung brought his classification into relation with his own doctrine of the unconscious, by suggesting a compensatory relation between the conscious and the unconscious in respect to type and the primary functions of the mind (thought, feeling, sensation, intuition). In its later formulation, this aspect of his theory does not have the significance in describing deviant behavior that it originally appeared to have, but it has greater significance as a part of his general theory of the mind and his special doctrine of the unconscious as it relates itself to the more complex aspects of his thought.

Step by step, Jung was thus led to the formulation of a new system of analytic doctrine, much more complicated than the Freudian and much more comprehensive and positively oriented on the cultural side. Recognizing this, he has termed his system "analytical psychology" in order to differentiate it from Freud's. It is evident that Jung's new viewpoint affected the whole structure of analytic doctrine, so that it has gradually led to a reinterpretation of most of the crucial concepts and principles of the Freudian system.

On the side of technique, Jung varied his procedure correspondingly. Apart from his reinterpretation of the content and scope of analytic material, in accordance with his extended concepts of libido and the unconscious and his emphasis on the study of personality type, he gradually altered the specific objectives of his procedure. He began to lay increasing emphasis on the analysis of present difficulties as against the probing into infantile history, on a more active type of therapy as against the passive concern of psychoanalysis with emotional release merely, and on the "synthetic" method as supplementary to the Freudian purely analytic method.

The latter point is highly important in Jung's therapy and

requires some explanation. The aim of therapy, according to him, is adjustment not analysis merely, and to achieve this larger aim, a synthetic approach is necessary beyond the purely analytic approach of Freud. The tearing down process of analysis, Jung maintained, must be followed by a building up process, the goal of which is the constructive reintegration of the patient's personality on a higher plane of development. For this, the analytic method must be supplemented by the synthetic method, which seeks to view the personality not reductively and retrospectively in terms of historical origins, neurotic mechanisms, and pathological symptoms, but constructively and prospectively in terms of strivings, aspirations, and potentialities for further growth. From the standpoint of the larger aim of adjustment, according to his position, analysis, which is concerned with the freeing of repressed libido, is merely the first step, and only the lesser part of the task. The more important part is the constructive guiding of the patient to a proper utilization of his newly released energy, and this means finally, from his standpoint, a better balanced philosophy of life and a higher moral and religious organization of the personality. For it is in respect to these aspects of development especially, according to his view, that modern man reveals his disorientation. This view he has suggestively expressed in the title of one of his later works—*Modern Man in Search of a Soul.*

In directing itself exclusively to the first part of the therapeutic task, psychoanalysis, according to Jung, fails to assume full therapeutic responsibility. It often leaves the patient in a state of helpless disorganization, the victim of released energy which has no constructive goal or direction. Some patients of exceptional inner strength are able to overcome this state of disorganization themselves, but in the case of those who cannot, psychoanalysis, according to him, reveals itself as not only inadequate but in many instances actually pernicious. The synthetic method directs itself to this problem and offers a solution through helping the patient to a positive reorganization of his personality, in terms of his revealed possibilities of further self-realization and development. Jung seeks to achieve this therapeutic aim by bringing the patient into active relation with his collective unconscious, a level of reintegration, he held, beyond the possibilities of the analytic method alone as interpreted by Freud.

The concept of "depth" psychology accordingly took on a new dimension in conjunction with Jung's position, which has been the source of much controversy and misunderstanding. In view of the charge of obscurity which is frequently directed against Jung, his own summary of some of these points is given. He says:

> In any evaluation of history, the creative spirit seems to me to have the greatest meaning for life, and I am convinced that no insight into the past and no revival—however strong—of pathogenic, sickening memories can be as effective in freeing man from the grip of the past as the construction of something new. I am of course very well aware that, without insight into the past and without an integration of important memories that have been lost, something new and living can not be created. But I regard it both as a loss of time and a misleading prejudice to rummage in the past for alleged specific causes of illness; for neuroses—no matter what the original occasion may be from which they once arose—are conditioned and maintained by a wrong attitude, which is continually present and which, once it is recognized, must be corrected *now* and not in the early period of infancy. Further, it is not enough merely to bring the causes into consciousness, for the cure of neuroses is, in the last analysis, a moral problem and not the magic effect of the revival of memories.[8]

Here, as so frequently in his theory, Jung sought to harmonize the viewpoint of Freud with that of Adler. Nevertheless, we are dealing, in his case, with a fundamentally different outlook

---

[8] W. M. Kranefeldt, *Secret Ways of the Mind*, pp. xxxiv-xxxv.

which is characteristic. As has already been noted, Jung recognized a primary spiritual striving in opposition to the sexual striving which Freud described. It is this creative, spiritual striving which his synthetic method seeks to mobilize and utilize constructively. This introduces an educational and moral or religious aspect to his procedure, which seemed especially objectionable to Freud, who criticised it as a surrender to convention and as an attempt to court popular favor through the injection of lofty ideas into the analytic process. Freud maintained that Jung ceased to be an analyst and that he made common cause with religious mysticism. Jung, on the other hand, stated that not only is the constructive part of his therapy empirically grounded just as the analytic part, but also, that it is a *vital necessity* from the therapeutic standpoint, if the disorganizing effects of analysis alone are to be avoided.[4] It is notable that Freud himself gradually incorporated this moral viewpoint into his system in the form of his doctrine of the super-ego.

But the interpretation which this viewpoint received at the hands of Freud merely emphasizes the fundamentally different outlook of their respective positions. Viewing the matter historically, Jung pointed out that before Freud nothing was allowed to be sexual; with him everything became "nothing but" sexual.[5] The latter position, he felt, represents a reaction against the former and reactions are known to be extreme. The Freudians, according to him, look upon the world in terms of the sex doctrine as through colored glasses; everything is colored by the theory. All differences are obliterated by it, no matter how significant. Religion, poetry, art—are these to be viewed as "nothing but" sublimations of repressed sexuality? he asks repeatedly. What about grandeur, beauty, nobility, holiness? Is anything to be gained by viewing them in the same terms as a neurotic symptom? Do we get an integrating world outlook from this view, insight, understanding, and appreciation of all

4 *Collected Papers on Analytical Psychology*, p. xv.
5 *Contributions to Analytical Psychology*, p. 347.

that is most worth while in life? Is not the Freudian viewpoint helpless in dealing with these highest products of the creative imagination?

It is in this concern with higher values in and for themselves, as of primary and not merely derived significance, that we have the parting of the ways between Freud and Jung. From this major point of departure, most of the important detailed differences pf Jung's position follow, complicated by a theory of the unconscious which is characteristically his own. This Freud himself clearly recognized. He said: "All the changes that Jung has wrought in psychoanalysis flow from the ambition to eliminate all that is disagreeable in the family complexes, so that it may not evidence itself again in ethics and religion."[6] This does not, however, invalidate Jung's position. It only indicates that psychoanalytic doctrine is as yet not freed from strong personal elements. Both Freud and Jung, in their separate ways, recognized this.[7]

---

[6] *Collected Papers,* vol. I, p. 353.

[7] Despite his concern with cultural materials, Jung, like Freud, failed to appreciate the developing contents of modern cultural anthropology and sociology. On that account, his thought incorporates a biological mysticism which he might have avoided, if he had been more familiar with these areas of investigation. Nevertheless, he introduced highly important considerations into analytic thought, which no amount of adverse methodological criticism can obscure.

Chapter IV

THE ADLERIAN BACKGROUND—INDIVIDUAL PSYCHOLOGY

Alfred Adler belonged to Freud's earliest circle of direct associates. For a time he worked harmoniously with Freud, but more dramatically even than in the case of C. G. Jung, a basically different viewpoint finally brought him into open conflict with the Freudian position. This occurred in 1911 in connection with Adler's emphasis on ego psychology in contrast with Freud's libido psychology. Since this was long before Freud had worked out his own theory of the structure of the personality in terms of id, ego, and super-ego, the difference of viewpoint was clear-cut. Significantly enough, Adler designated his system "individual psychology," thus cutting off completely from the background term "psychoanalysis."

Adler did not deny the importance of the sex impulse any more than did Jung, but like Jung, he did not believe it had the dominating significance attributed to it by Freud. According to Adler, it takes its place in the total pattern of life and is to be viewed in relation to the development of the total personality. And the latter seemed to him to be basically determined by the ego principles of self-preservation and self-assertion, termed by him, in their more aggressive aspects, "the will to power." Sex difficulties in neurotic patients, which Freud stressed so much, Adler gradually came to view as only a symptomatic and symbolic expression of a more basic personality difficulty which he described as the "feeling of inferiority" and the compensatory "striving for superiority." Inferiority feeling, which is the common lot of mankind in childhood, according to him, gives rise inevitably to the compensatory striving for superiority as the response of personality to dependency, insecurity, and disappointment. In more extreme cases, accentuated inferiority feeling gives rise to an "inferiority complex" and to an intensified striving for power which, not being realizable in most instances, leads to "fictive arrangements" in support of place, prestige, and power. Thus the stage is set for those many-sided mechanisms of evasion, compensation, and overcompensation, which Adler described and analyzed with such impressive detail.

More specifically, according to Adler, inferiority feeling has its origin in the helplessness of the child. From this point, the individual develops into a normal or pathological human being, in accordance with the types of compensation which he adopts and the goal of superiority striving which he sets for himself. As long as one's striving for superiority is compatible with social life, the individual remains within the limits of what is considered normal; when the superiority striving comes into conflict with social standards and requirements, the individual passes increasingly beyond socially acceptable limits and eventually may become disordered. The normal person, in his striving for superiority, is directed along constructive social lines through the cultivation of social feeling and cooperation; the neurotic is egocentric and inadequately socialized and hence, tends to come into conflict with the norms of social life. This accentuates his inferiority feeling and intensifies his striving for superiority, so that they become ever less compatible with reality. He is thus forced to retreat into a "fictive" world and to take refuge in imaginary compensations for his constantly increasing feeling of inferiority and his correspondingly intensified drive for power. "The will to power" becomes "the will to seem powerful" and the individual finds himself in the whirlpool of the proverbial vicious circle.[1]

Elaborated by Adler in his various works through frequent repetition and striking illustration, this train of thought has achieved a popularity rivaled only by the more spectacular aspects of Freudian doctrine itself. The familiarity of the concepts "inferiority complex" and "superiority complex" and, in lesser degree, also of the dramatic concept "the masculine protest," another expression for "the will to power," is an indication of the extent to which Adler's views have entered into popular thought.

Freud, when he came to the formulation of his ego doctrine, related the ego with the "reality principle." In contrast Adler, in working out his position, increasingly emphasized the special tendency of the ego to fall into disharmony with reality as a manner of evading responsibility and falsely winning a privileged position in life, as a defense adjustment, that is, to the feeling of inferiority and the compensatory striving for superiority. This is a fundamental point of difference between Adlerian and Freudian theory and from it issue most of the specific details characterizing Adler's deviant views.

Adler first worked out the essentials of his position on a physical basis, in terms of organ inferiority, but he gradually elaborated his theory in purely psychological terms. Eventually, it assumed the importance of a general principle of psychological explanation corresponding to Freud's sexual doctrine. At first it seemed that these two principles of explanation were

[1] It is revealing to compare this conception with Freud's view of neurosis as due chiefly to repression and with Jung's view, according to which it is primarily the result of one-sided and hence unbalanced development. Conceptions of therapy correspond: the Freudian emphasizing the freeing of repressions; the Jungian, the realignment of developmental capacities; the Adlerian, the socialization of the individual's behavior pattern.

merely two aspects of the same situation and many, including Jung, attempted to reconcile them. But in the course of time, as Adler developed his theory and built up a comprehensive system of thought around it, the difference of viewpoint stood out ever more prominently. Adler, in particular, maintained that the two positions are irreconcilable, since, according to him, his theory incorporates not merely differences in detail of explanation but a basically different conception of personality and behavior, and even a fundamentally different philosophy of life.

In its developed form, Adler's theory stresses, besides the above, such concepts as family background and sibling order, style of life, goal, and social adjustment, especially in the form of co-operation and social interest. The significance of the shift of perspective which these concepts represent, consists in the fact that it brings the unified personality into view as a primary consideration as against the atomistic drive mechanisms of Freud's theory. An analysis of the individual in terms of sex, according to Adler, gives not only a one-sided picture, as Jung maintained, for example, but also a distorted and erroneous picture, since the sex aspect of behavior, according to him, like any other aspect, can be correctly viewed only in terms of the unified personality as expressed in its goal patterns and conception of life.

"All psychical phenomena," says Adler, "originate in the particular creative force of the individual, and are expressions of his personality."[2] Over and over again, he points to the doctrine of "the unity of the personality" as a basic principle of interpretation.[3] In other words, sex is a function of personality, not the other way around. That, in fact, is the real significance of "individual psychology" as the term is used by Adler. He stressed the need of studying the total personality as a dynamic and indivisible unity in respect to all the manifestations of behavior, and furthermore, in intimate positive interrelation with

[2] Carl Murchison (ed.), *Psychologies of 1930,* "*Individual Psychology,*" p. 397.
[3] *The Practice and Theory of Individual Psychology,* pp. 2-4.

the social setting, more particularly, the immediate social background represented by family and other direct associates. In this, he is on common ground with Gestalt psychology and other integrative developments in modern psychological and social thought, particularly social psychology.

In its general orientation at least, therefore, Adler brought his theory into closer relation with general psychological and social theory than most analysts, though Jung's theory also represents a departure in the direction of a more integrated and social, especially cultural interpretation of behavior. Nevertheless, Adler's theory has seemed to illustrate peculiarly the narrow foundation of a good deal of analytic doctrine and its extension beyond the scope of the considered evidence. As organ inferiority, his theory was definite and specific. Developed in purely psychological terms, it became vague and indefinite. For the interpretation of inferiority in purely psychic terms presents anew the whole problem of studying the specific conditions under which such inferiority feeling develops and the approach by way of organ defect loses its special significance.

However, as Jung observed, Adler's contributions have been decisive, especially in that his theory was among the first to challenge fundamentally the fixity of Freudian doctrine.For it provides an alternative viewpoint which has been widely influential even in the development of psychoanalytic doctrine itself, notably in connection with Freud's later formulation of ego psychology, the castration doctrine, and his later aggression theory.[4]

In respect to technique, as is to be expected, Adler diverged

---

[4] In addition to Freudian doctrine and his own original work on organ inferiority, Adler was greatly influenced in his views by Marxian theory, his position, at some points, being practically a translation of Marxian thought on class conflict applied on the level of individual behavior. In this respect, Adler's position represents an integration of two of the most dynamic viewpoints in nineteenth century thought: the Freudian and the Marxian. And curiously, the result of his combination of the two systems of thought which stressed conflict so much, both group and individual, was a special emphasis on social interest and cooperation as the only means by which mental health and social adjustment can be secured in human society.

even more widely from the orthodox Freudian procedure than Jung. Both the content and handling of material are radically altered. Adler dispensed with some of the most distinctive features of the Freudian analysis: the special physical setting, the concentrated concern with the unconscious, the cultivation of the transference, the therapeutic emphasis on resistance and repression. Free association, dream analysis, and interpretation are all distinctively oriented in his own viewpoint. In particular, the goal and style of life are emphasized, especially the manner of adjustment to the three critical problems represented by social life, vocation, and marriage, or more broadly, love. The analytic process, in his case, becomes essentially an educational and guidance procedure, the objective of which is the re-education of the patient into a more socially directed pattern of life, through persuasion, encouragement, the development of insight and, above all, the cultivation of an interest on the part of the patient in acquiring co-operative habits of thought and behavior.

Adler says in this connection:

Individual psychology considers the essence of therapy to lie in making the patient aware of his lack of co-operative power, and to convince him of the origin of this lack in early childhood maladjustments. What passes during this process is no small matter; his power of co-operation is enhanced by collaboration with the doctor. His "inferiority complex" is revealed as erroneous. Courage and optimism are awakened. And the "meaning of life" dawns upon him as the fact that proper meaning must be given to life.[5]

He further states:

The aim of this point of view is to gain a reinforced sense of reality, the development of a feeling of responsibility and a substitute for latent hatred of a feeling of mutual

[5] Carl Murchison (ed.), *Psychologies of 1930*, "Individual Psychology," p. 404.

good-will, all of which can be gained only by the conscious evolution of a feeling for the common weal and the conscious destruction of the will-to-power.[6]

It is clear from the above that Adler's approach is thoroughly synthetic and constructive. Also, that in connection with his central concept of "goal," he places emphasis on the prospective viewpoint as necessary, in addition to the retrospective historical viewpoint. In fact, as has been noted, Jung's departure in these directions had its roots in Adler's position, Jung's expressed aim, in this respect, having been to harmonize the viewpoints of Freud and Adler.

The Freudians have criticised Adler on many grounds but especially on the ground that his procedure is superficial, since it does not attempt to get at what they understand by "depth" psychology. Adler, on the other hand, presented a fundamental criticism of the Freudian position and his defenders have suggested, in effect, that his procedure is "deeper" than the Freudian, in the only sense in which "depth" has any significance, namely, that it is based on a better grasp of the actual functioning personality. In this controversy, Jung has sought to maintain an intermediate position, recognizing the viewpoints of both Freud and Adler in part, but holding that both are one-sided and in themselves inadequate. In his own doctrine, Jung has accordingly sought to give place to both positions, but in addition, he has introduced novel elements of his own which have, in turn, been the source of adverse comment and counter criticism.[7]

There is, of course, no simple way of checking these claims and counter-claims in the analytic field. But the conclusion is

[6] *The Practice and Theory of Individual Psychology*, p. 14.

[7] Of the two departures represented by Jung and Adler, Freud regarded Adler's as "indubitably the more significant." While he stated that it was "radically false" and had "nothing to do with psychoanalysis," he felt that it was at least "marked by consistence and coherence," whereas Jung's doctrine, in attempting to incorporate inharmonious elements, according to him, is confused and tends to vacillate from page to page. (*Collected Papers*, vol. 1, pp. 347, 350.)

inescapable from a comparative consideration of the Freudian, Jungian, and Adlerian systems, that psychotherapy, in its present stage of development, is apparently not tied to any single system of theory or procedure, since it may be carried on, with some measure of success, in terms of such widely differentiated viewpoints and under such widely diverse conditions. What this means for all of the systems considered remains a problem for continuing investigation. But meanwhile the problem is noted here and it will be brought into further historical perspective in the discussion of the Rankian position.

Part III

Essentials of Rank's
Psychology and Psychotherapy

Chapter V

RANK'S WILL OR DYNAMIC RELATIONSHIP THERAPY[1]

Otto Rank, as was described in the opening chapter of this survey, was also one of Freud's early associates in the field of psychoanalysis. However, he remained with Freud for more than a decade after Jung and Adler had come into open conflict with Freud's views. In the course of his many years of association with Freud, and especially during the period following the separation of Jung and Adler from the psychoanalytic group, Rank's thought absorbed elements from each of their systems. These elements he gradually worked into a distinctive viewpoint of his own and particularly a distinctive therapeutic viewpoint. It is notable, in this connection, that his point of departure from the Freudian position was, in the first place, not in respect to a question of theoretical interpretation, as was the case with Jung and Adler, but rather in respect to the fundamental issue of the relation of theory and therapy as a whole, as already suggested in the discussion of the Adlerian position.

In the Freudian system, theory and therapy are so intimately

[1] See explanatory footnote p. 21 regarding Dr. Rank's cooperation in the original preparation of this outline of his essential views on therapy.

interrelated that they seem to be inseparable. In 1922 Rank raised the question as to whether this is justified, in view of the different theoretical viewpoints current in the field, and whether it does not lead to unnecessary confusion, both in respect to analytic theory and therapy, to consider them so closely interlinked.[2] Next, in collaboration with Sandor Ferenczi, another fundamental issue was brought into view, at least in incipient form, the question of activity and passivity in therapy, later developed by Rank in connection with his special device of setting a time limit in the analytic situation.[3] The final break with the Freudian group came as a result of the publication of the *Trauma of Birth in* 1924, which appeared to bring the basic orientation of Freudian theory into question, with central reference to the interpretation of the important problem of anxiety and related therapeutic problems.[4]

[2] The period following the separation of Jung and Adler was one of restless ferment in the psychoanalytic movement as well as general disillusionment, even insofar as Freud himself was concerned. With the elaboration of psychoanalytic theory, psychoanalytic procedure was constantly being lengthened and, correspondingly, the procedure was limited to a reduced number of patients. This was disturbing to all of the leaders of the movement, including Freud. It was Rank's conviction that the constant lengthening of the psychoanalytic process was due to the requirements of psychoanalytic investigation as comprehended by Freud, and was not an essential part of effective therapy. It was on this account, that he raised the fundamental issue of the interrelation of psychoanalytic theory and therapy. (*The Development of Psychoanalysis,* p. 2; *The Trauma of Birth,* p. 202; *Will Therapy,* p. 11.)

[3] Ferenczi and Rank developed their views on "activity" in different directions following their collaboration on *The Development of Psychoanalysis,* Ferenczi having become more actively directive than Rank, who limited himself to manipulation of the therapeutic situation, particularly in terms of end-setting and such auxiliary factors as the physical arrangement of the patient and therapist which, as he believed, had accidently and arbitrarily become associated with psychoanalytic therapy. (*The Development of Psychoanalysis,* pp. 4-5; *The Trauma of Birth,* p. 203; *Will Therapy,* pp. 10, 21.)

[4] Following the Freudian pattern, Rank first formulated his birth trauma theory in biological terms. But the theory was based on therapeutic observations and cultural study and the biological formulation was a superstructure not at all a necessary part of the theory. Gradually, he accordingly discarded the questionable biological aspects of his theory and directed himself increasingly to the elaboration of the psychological and therapeutic aspects. That this work nevertheless precipitated intense controversy has already been noted. This was apart

From that time on, Rank developed his divergent position in many directions, especially in the following publications: *Outlines of a Genetic Psychology* (in two parts or volumes and as yet published only in German); *Art and Artist* (which is available in English); *Modern Education* (which is also available in English); and particularly in his *Technique of Psychoanalysis* (in three parts or volumes, the second and third of which have been translated into English under the title *Will Therapy*); also in a philosophical discussion entitled *Truth and Reality* (which was originally presented as the third part of his *Outlines of a Genetic Psychology* but is an independent work and appears as such in English.) [5]

Like Jung and Adler, Rank found it necessary to develop a new set of categories in order to formulate his position, and such others as he took over, he found it necessary to reinterpret basically. His *post-Trauma of Birth* formulations stress the following conceptions as especially important for an understanding of his position: impulse, inhibition, and will as basic categories of interpretation; anxiety, fear, guilt, and denial as distinctive points of departure in the development of his position; the artistic, neurotic, and anti-social (criminal and psychopathic) types, viewed by him as corresponding, in respect to pattern of personality organization, to his basic categories of interpretation; and finally, more specifically insofar as his therapeutic position is concerned, the analytic situation and the therapist and neurotic types in their therapeutic relationship,

---

from the particular doctrine advanced which, as it happened, was not completely unfamiliar to Freudian thought. Its special psychoanalytic threat was interpreted as following from its indirect challenge to the primacy of the Freudian Oedipus doctrine which was replaced by the birth trauma theory as the primary principle of interpretation. The broad cultural implications of this basic shift of orientation in Rank's attempt to reinterpret psychoanalytic doctrine are developed in Chapter VII.

[5] A posthumously published volume, entitled *Beyond Psychology* (1941), appeared since the original formulation of this discussion and likewise a translation of a suggestive work entitled *Psychology and the Soul* (1950).

viewed by him as the essential factors in the therapeutic process.[6]

In the above-mentioned works, Rank presents a detailed study of the artistic and neurotic types—the one especially in his *Art and Artist,* the other in his *Technique;* a detailed analysis of the dynamics of the analytic process, most systematically developed in his *Technique;* a developmental formulation of his general psychological position as projected upon the background of Freudian doctrine in his *Trauma of Birth* and in his *Genetic Psychology* and, in broader scope, in his *Truth and Reality;* and applications of his viewpoint in various directions, notably in his *Art and Artist* and his *Modern Education.*

Rank's early work dealt with the analytic interpretation of culture forms, especially art, mythology, and literature. He accordingly brought an exceptionally broad social and cultural outlook and background to the treatment of special analytic problems. It is particularly important to note this in attempting to estimate his position. Both Jung and Adler, it will be recalled, departed from Freud in the direction of a broader social and cultural viewpoint, but in the case of both of them, this viewpoint was rooted in the biological perspective and secondary. In the case of Rank, it was a direct outgrowth of his early work and much more basic. On the other hand, his longtime intimate association with Freud gave him a keen grasp of crucial analytic issues related to the investigation of the individual from the Freudian biological viewpoint. This made for a balancing of perspectives which finally led Rank to a conception of the functional interrelation of the individual and the social in behavior that, until recently, was unique in analytic doctrine and that historically has set his work off as a distinctive contribution to the field.

[6] The subtitle and the three parts of his *Technique* stress these essential factors. The entire work is concerned with the analysis of the therapeutic process in terms of relationship, as stated in the subtitle, and the three parts deal respectively with the following subject-matter: The Analytic Situation in Part I, The Analytic Reaction in Part II, The Analyst and His Role in Part III.

Insofar as Rank's general background is concerned, it is only necessary at this point, to add a comment about his special emphasis on the concept of will. This concept is central in his theoretical formulation and is related to his study of the creative personality and the creative aspect of behavior generally. In his therapeutic use of this term, he has reference to nothing mystical, as the term itself might suggest, but only to the dynamic organization of the personality for the achievement of some objective.[7] Concretely, in the analytic situation, for example, he has reference to "the will to health," or the dynamic organization of the personality for the achievement of the health objective, which objective, quite obviously, is common to both patient and therapist. The task of therapy, from this standpoint, it should be noted, is essentially one of positive will organization and mobilization or, more familiarly, of the strengthening of the positive side of personality.[8]

In this connection, and, in fact, quite generally in his discussion of the will concept, he stressed creativity as the important consideration, not in any secondary or supplementary sense, as is most frequently the case in biologically oriented analytic discussions, but as a primary consideration and as the central point of attack in the therapeutic handling of the personality. The neurotic, according to Rank, is basically a creative type, but negative and destructive in expression.[9] The therapeutic task,

7 "I understand by will," says Rank, "a positive guiding organization and integration of self which utilizes creatively, as well as inhibits and controls the instinctual drives." (*Will Therapy*, p. 158). He also states: "For me the problem of willing, in a philosophical sense of the word, had come to be the central problem of the whole question of personality, even of all psychology". (*Art and Artist*, p. 9.) Will, as Rank uses the term concretely in therapy, accordingly refers to the organized and integrated personality in decisive, creative, and self-assertive action. And will therapy refers to the process of will strengthening under the conditions operative in the therapeutic situation.

8 *Will Therapy*, chap. II, *Truth and Reality*, chap. II.

9* Rank identifies the neurotic type with the "artiste manqué," the artistic temperament which fails to attain artistic expression. The neurotic thus represents, according to him, not so much a failure in normal development as a failure in creativity. (*Art and Artist*, chaps. I and II.) This conception and Rank's corresponding view of therapy may be compared with the other positions considered. (See note p. 41.)

therefore, is to secure a more positive and constructive expression of the personality, and this problem in turn, as already suggested, is from his standpoint essentially a problem of positive will or personality organization.

It is evident that the will concept plays a similar role in Rank's doctrine that the concepts of goal and will-to-power play in Adlerian doctrine, but he used it to give greater emphasis to the positive aspects of personality expression. It is clear also that this concept, as used by Rank, presents inherently a unified, synthetic, and constructive view of behavior, so that he has no need to direct special attention to these aspects of the situation in a secondary or supplementary sense, as is the case in Jungian and even in Adlerian doctrine. All in all, he places emphasis in terms of his will concept on the active, positive, integrative, and creative aspects of behavior in the sense of active self-expression and control of adjustment, in contrast to the passive, negative, and deterministic aspects stressed in Freudian doctrine and, to a lesser extent, also in Jungian and Adlerian doctrine.

Freudian theory, according to Rank, has become a philosophy of despair in its emphasis on blind force, as appears strikingly in its doctrine of the "death instinct." In terms of his will doctrine, Rank opposes to this conception his own view of active adjustment, which should not be strange to American students who are acquainted with American psychological and social thought of the late nineteenth and early twentieth centuries, despite the unfamiliar setting which he gives his doctrine and also despite the unfamiliar spirit in which he develops it, insofar as his reference to philosophic sources is concerned, which are not primary in American thought. The individual, according to him, and in agreement with traditional American thought quite generally, does not merely adapt himself passively to his environment; he also controls, directs, and moulds it. He is not merely a passive factor in the adaptive process; he is also in some sense, as has been familiarly said, "master of his fate."[9]

It is this active control side of adjustment which Rank's will doctrine seeks to lay hold of and to make central in therapy. What is passively determined in behavior, we cannot do anything about, according to Rank, but what is an expression of active will, is open to constructive manipulation and we can direct it to our purpose. It then only becomes a question as to whose purpose should predominate. In this respect, Rank's position differs strikingly from the other positions considered in his emphasis on the neurotic type as a unique and distinctive and creative type of personality and in his opposition, therefore, to what he termed "normative" and "ideological" or predetermined patterns of therapy, characteristics which, according to him, particularly describe psychoanalytic procedure in its later development.

Believing in creative therapy, in therapy as essentially an "art," Rank was naturally not interested in technique in the narrow sense of specific rules of procedure.[10] Despite the Ger-

---

[9] Rank's formulations must always be viewed in terms of his Freudian background. In connection with his use of the term will, he aimed to avoid the Freudian departmentalized view of personality, and so he opposed it with his unifying concept of will. That Rank's will theory likewise seems unfamiliar to modern psychological thought is a limitation of the situation and the psychology of his time. It is evident from Rank's general discussion and therapeutic emphasis, however, that what he was after was the sort of dynamic, organized, and integrated view of behavior which is commonly expressed today in terms of personality theory. His general conception of will is not unlike the treatment incorporated in James' *Psychology* and Rank introduced the will concept for the same essential reasons that James did, namely, opposition to a completely atomistic, mechanistic, and deterministic view of personality and conduct. The similarity is not altogether accidental, for Rank came under the influence of a European pragmatist during his student days and, in this way, he became acquainted with James' thought.

[10] Rank said in this connection: "The presentation of a psychotherapeutic technique, as I understand it, comprises, then, neither the general norm-setting theory formation, no matter from where it comes or of what kind it is, nor yet the enumeration of a set of practical rules and prescriptions such as Freud attempted bit by bit. One can modify these rules or turn them into the opposite or entirely ignore them and still get results; just as one can fail while observing

man title of his work, he accordingly stated in his *Will Therapy:* "I have attempted to write in place of a technique of psychotherapy, a 'Philosophy of Helping,' without which an understanding of any kind of psychotherapy or technique seems to me to be impossible." In this broader sense of a philosophy of the helping process, then, the chief points of his departure in respect to procedure may be briefly summarized as follows:

(1) His general viewpoint, as described in terms of his will theory, which provides the framework for his distinctive conception of the analytic process and for his emphasis on "relationship" as the determining aspect of the process. This conception brings into focus the other key concept of Rank's psychotherapy, alongside of the central will concept, namely relationship, the former being featured in the title and the latter in the subtitle of his *Will Therapy*. This accounts for the double designation of Rank's position in terms of "will" and "relationship" in this survey and elsewhere.[11]

(2) His emphasis on the emotional dynamics of the analytic situation as the essential therapeutic agent and, more specifically, on "experiencing" in the analytic situation as against learning in the intellectual sense, recall, making conscious, giving insight by theoretical interpretation, and the like.

(3) His orientation of the analytic process in the present and particularly in the analytic situation, in contrast to the Freud-

---

them strictly. Everything depends on the understanding and correct management of the therapeutic situation and this lies in the essential understanding and guiding of the individual reactions of the patient," that is, in the patient-therapist "relationship" which Rank accordingly stressed as the central therapeutic theme in his *Will Therapy*. (*Will Therapy,* p. 7.)

11 The therapeutic concept of relationship, as understood by Rank, is a direct outgrowth of his "birth trauma" theory and his resulting view of the patient-therapist relationship as a "libidinal bond to the mother" in place of the Freudian father-centered transference conception with its guiding reference to the Oedipus complex. This basic shift of orientation which, as already noted, precipitated Rank's break with the Freudian group and eventually resulted in a many-sided attempt to reinterpret psychoanalytic theory and therapy, is too complicated for further comment at this point. It will be dealt with at greater length in several later connections.

ian probing into the infantile past, and in contrast also to the supplementary emphasis on the future in the case of Adler and on present problems in the case of Jung. The latter, it should be noted, differs from Rank's emphasis on the present in that it centers attention on adjustment problems outside of the analytic situation.

(4) In this connection and also more generally as a part of his will doctrine, Rank stressed the need of grasping the new elements in the therapeutic situation as against the Freudian interest in infantile reproduction, since therapy must obviously, according to him, be effected in terms of what is new in the therapeutic situation rather than in terms of what is old and a matter of behavior repetitions.

(5) Associated with this viewpoint, is a shift of emphasis from specific content, that is, from the need of reliving individual experiences in detail, to form or pattern of reaction, to the dynamics underlying specific content, or to what Rank described suggestively as the "algebra" in contrast to the "arithmetic" of the situation.[12]

(6) His special device of end-setting which had high historical importance in the development of his distinctive position and also general significance in that it links up with the larger previously mentioned question of activity and passivity in the therapeutic situation.

Rank early became concerned with the device of setting a "time limit" in the analytic process, in order to bring under the control of the analytic situation the end phase of the therapeutic process and the solution of the important problem of separation which it precipitates in dramatic form and which he considered basic in the process of therapeutic as well as general adjustment. The setting of a time limit projects the end phase

12 This conception, taken in conjunction with his resulting disregard of specific content, especially content dealing with the infantile period, and his use of the time limit, enabled Rank to develop a shortened form of analytic therapy, long before its recent more general popularity. This became one of the identifying features and most controversial aspects of his procedure.

forward, so that it makes possible a gradual and more adequate solution of the separation problem and the termination phase of the therapeutic process.[13]

(7) This leads to the next and, according to Rank, especially important point, namely, his emphasis on the will aspects of the analytic process and on the constructive utilization of the creative elements in the therapeutic situation, as already noted above.

As might be expected from what has already been said on this point, Rank stressed the need of adapting the situation to the unique individual needs of each patient. The process, according to him, must be patient-centered not therapist-centered; it must be flexible, adaptable, constructive, alert to the new and unexpected; a genuinely creative experience for both patient and therapist. The neurotic personality, according to him, can never be fitted into the average norm, since it is by nature different in that it represents the creative type. Therapy must direct itself to this basic fact and lead the patient to realize himself in his own terms. The function of therapy, then, is not to determine the content of the therapeutic process, but so to manipulate the dynamics of the will-relationship automatically set up in the analytic situation, whatever the content as determined by the patient, as to strengthen the positive side of the patient's personality, with a view to enabling him increasingly to take over constructive management of himself in the analytic situation and, thereby, increasingly also in his life situation. Eventually, if this task is successfully carried out, the

[13] Activity and passivity, the time limit, separation and termination, like the more general therapeutic concept of relationship, are all concepts of deep theoretical and therapeutic significance in Rank's psychotherapy and they all link up with his trauma of birth doctrine which, in its most controversial aspects, appeared to attack the primacy of the Freudian Oedipus complex and to shift instead to a mother-centered interpretation of anxiety and dependency. In his later formulations, Rank tended to interpret these concepts on the psychological and social plane in terms of his will psychology and relationship therapy. (*Will Therapy*, chaps. II, VII; *Truth and Reality*, chaps. I, VI; *Beyond Psychology*, chap. IV.)

patient will reach a point when he will be ready to dispense with the artificial assistance of the therapeutic situation and thus he will determine the natural ending of the process, not in terms of preconceived content, but in terms of the dynamics of the situation and the developing needs of the patient, regarded by Rank as a self-reliant and self-responsible person.

That this conception of therapy places a heavier burden on the therapist than most conceptions, since he is thrown so much on his own resources, was readily admitted by Rank. But he maintained that the apt therapist should himself be of the creative type, and moreover positive in expression, in order that he might function as the necessary positive complement to the patient who is maladjusted because he is negative in expression. In that case, the therapist will but find scope for his own creative expression in the therapeutic situation so conceived. In the dramatic interplay of personalities which takes place in the therapeutic situation, both therapist and patient can thus come to creative self-realization. This is certainly an inspiring, if not always achievable view of therapy. The usual situation approaches this ideal to a greater or lesser extent in accordance with the creative possibilities of the personalities involved.

(8) It is interesting to note in conjunction with Rank's will conception of the therapeutic process, inasmuch as it epitomizes his distinctive position, that he arrived at his basic will concept from a study of resistance, just as Freud arrived at his basic concept of repression from a study of this phenomenon. According to Rank, resistance is not merely a hindrance to therapy, as psychoanalysis views it, but it is a negative will expression which, from a positive standpoint, expresses a constructive striving toward independence and hence should be encouraged, strengthened, and directed, not undermined as in psychoanalytic procedure. In fact, according to him, no really constructive therapeutic result is possible without some regard to this more positive view of the situation. In this difference of outlook and conception, we have the historical germ of his distinctive position

and therapeutic procedure, as they were elaborated since his departure from orthodox Freudian theory and therapy.[14]

(9) An additional important point must be mentioned by way of bringing to a head Rank's therapeutic position in its social aspects, namely, his conception of the interdependent relation of the individual and the social order in which the individual comes to self-realization. In this respect, as in respect to his will doctrine in its bearing on his view of active adjustment and his conception of resistance as negative will expression, his position differs radically from the Freudian position. In effect, he replaces the Freudian antithetical view of individual libido striving and social restriction with a view of the dynamic interdependent relation of the individual and the social world, which essentially reflects the position of modern social psychology, especially in its earlier phases of development.[15]

The social world cannot, from his standpoint, be chiefly regarded as a limitation on libido striving, for it is also the necessary condition for libido expression. The individual, according to him, needs society for his own harmonious development and self-realization. There is, then, no question of the opposition of the individual to the social world in the Freudian sense, but only of their constructive interrelation. The social world, he points out in various connections, is a part of the individual and the individual is a part of the social world; neither exists in isolation or in complete opposition to the other.

"The human being," says Rank, "is not only an individual but also a social being."[16] He also states: "The ego needs the

[14] It has already been noted in connection with "relationship" that Rank likewise reinterpreted the psychoanalytic concept of transference basically. In terms of will and relationship, therefore, Rank attacked the "two observed facts" of psychoanalysis which, according to Freud, constitute the distinguishing feature of psychoanalytic therapy. (*Collected Papers*, vol. I, p. 298.)

[15] *Art and Artist*, chap. I; *Will Therapy*, Book II, chap. VII; *Truth and Reality*, chap. I; *Beyond Psychology*, chaps. I, III, IV. Cf. Karpf, *American Social Psychology*, especially Part II.

[16] *Will Therapy*, p. 287.

Thou in order to become a Self" and similarly "the psychology of the Self is to be found in the Other, be that Other the individual Thou, or the inspirational ideology of the leader, or the symbiotic diffusion of another civilization."[17] It is a theme which Rank develops in various directions, in its individual, social, and collective aspects; in relation to art, education, therapy, psychology, and personality development.

The protoype of the relationship is to be seen in the mother-child relationship.[18] They form an interdependent dynamic unity which is vital; neither is complete without the other or apart from their unifying relationship. The relationship may be used constructively or destructively but that is another matter and, in the latter case, is a problem for therapy. Similarly in the therapeutic and larger social situation. There is no question of the therapeutic adaptation of a passive individual to a fixed social order termed "reality," but of their constructive interrelation, and this again may become a problem for therapy. From this standpoint, psychology becomes in a genuine sense *social* psychology, at least by implication, and psychotherapy becomes a somewhat questionable term, if it is associated with the traditional antithetical view of the individual and society. In any event, it is to be noted that Rank's position in this regard represents a radical departure from Freudian thought and is also a step beyond the social and cultural viewpoints of Jung and Adler. It is furthermore evident that his position, in its wider implcations, has a far-reaching significance for an understanding of his conception of the therapeutic relation, of the individual, society, and what, in the light of the above, are the complicated psychological and social problems of psychotherapy.

(10) But this position, in the case of Rank, must be viewed in conjunction with his constant emphasis on the unique, indi-

17 *Beyond Psychology*, p. 290.

18 In his later views, Rank rarely referred to his original birth trauma formulation of this conception but he stressed the psychological, therapeutic, and social reference of the conception.

vidual, and creative aspects of behavior. For it is characteristic of Rank's viewpoint that it is never one-sided but rests squarely, in his own words, "on two legs." As has already been indicated in a previous connection, this integrated two-sided viewpoint constituted one of his chief contributions to the field.

(11) Despite the fundamental character of these departures, Rank remained closer to the original purpose of the Freudian analysis than either Jung or Adler. For this reason, he was more directly active in reinterpreting the dynamics of the psychoanalytic process than either of them. For this reason, too, he has remained an active issue in the field, even insofar as orthodox Freudian procedure is concerned, as the others have not, and especially in this country, where Freudian thought seems to be more strongly intrenched than anywhere else. The meaning of the analytic process has been fundamentally redefined for Freudians as well as for others by Rank's thought-provoking innovations and formulations.[19]

Precisely because of this, however, Rank's position has been more exposed to critical attack than most analytically deviant positions. His views have long been and still remain the subject-matter of lively discussion and controversy. But this merely indicates the importance of some familiarity with the main features of his position and its relation to the various aspects of the currently active and developing field of psychotherapy.

(12) *Supplementary Note on Social Work:* In this country, Rank was from the first closely associated with the field of social work from which, as a center, his influence has extended into various other fields. This fact is important because, on the one hand, Rank's association with the field of social work has tended to confirm at once his social and individualized outlook and, on the other hand, the Freudian and Rankian positions being predominant in the field of social work, the rivalry of the two viewpoints has intensified and, at times, exaggerated antagonisms which might otherwise have been gradually reduced

[19] Cf. Clara Thompson, *Psychoanalysis, Evolution and Development,* chap. IX.

through mutually reinterpreted experiences. This is strikingly illustrated in a recent important publication entitled *A Comparison of Diagnostic and Functional Casework Concepts* (Family Service Association of America, 1950), which has stressed differences and subdued similarities to such an extent as to accent a definite cleavage or "schism" that seems to have developed between the Freudian-oriented and the Rankian-oriented groups in the social work field.

It is interesting to observe in this connection that the emotionally-charged type of discussion which has centered about this work and the situation to which it refers, appears to reproduce the controversial tone that has always characterized deviation from psychoanalytic theory and practice in the psychoanalytic movement itself. For some reason the pattern of fighting the whole world which was defensively adopted by Freud is automatically carried over by his adherents to every development associated with psychoanalysis. It is in part because of this that the deviant analytic positions are so important in preserving flexibility in the movement and the Rankian position, in this particular situation, especially. For otherwise, a single predominant and perhaps unchallenged viewpoint would control the field and this would be just as unwholesome in therapy in its present state of development, as a single state party in politics.[20]

---

20 This subject is further considered in the following chapter.

Chapter VI

DISTINCTIVE ASPECTS OF RANK'S PERSONALITY THEORY[1]

Like all theory which developed as an offshoot of psycho-analytic doctrine, Rank's theory of personality appears upon the established background of psychoanalytic thought and is presented chiefly by contrast with and frequently criticism of the Freudian position. As in the case of other such develop-ments, notably the theories of Jung and Adler, the emergence of Rank's distinctive viewpoint was a gradual process, the cumula-tive product, in his case, of a laborious course of differentiation and crystallization of conception in respect to specific problems and issues, such as were noted in the preceeding chapter. In the light of later events, some of his views took on special impor-tance and thereby gradually led to the formulation of a more integrated statement of position, with emphasis on the distinc-tive aspects of his thinking.

In his earlier discussions, Rank for the most part utilized the accepted terminology of Freudian theory. It is clear from

[1] This statement was in essence originally formulated shortly before Dr. Rank's sudden death. While the material has been expanded, it nevertheless pre-dominantly represents what is probably the last statement of his position made with his active cooperation. See explanatory footnotes pp. 21, 49.

the first, however, that this terminology appears in a basically different context which reflects an essentially different conception of personality and its functioning in social life. Accepted terms thus gradually took on a characteristic meaning and as, in the course of time, differences were sharpened, the adoption of a more distinctive terminology was the natural solution to a condition of ambiguity and confusion which was in the making for a period of two decades. (From 1905 when he completed his early psychoanalytic work, *Der Künstler*, to 1924 when the *Trauma of Birth* was published.)[2]

It has already been stated that Rank was one of Freud's early students and associates, and that he continued in close association with Freud for more than a decade after Jung and Adler had publicly come into conflict with him. In the course of this lengthy period of contact with Freud, and especially during the later decade of Freud's lively controversy with Jung and Adler, Rank's thinking and technical procedure incorporated elements from each of these analytic systems, while continuing to remain predominantly Freudian in interest and outlook. His viewpoint is, therefore, the most inclusive of this early group of analysts, though all of them, in their respective ways, have included elements from the others. Thus, he gave place in characteristic manner, alike to the constructive and synthetic emphasis of Jung as well as to the social reference of Adlerian doctrine, and at the same time, he retained both the general setting and chief emphasis of Freudian theory and therapy.

This must not be taken to mean, however, that his position is predominantly a composite of these other systems. For, as already suggested, he worked these and other background elements into a distinctive viewpoint of his own which, for the above reasons, it is at times quite as necessary to differentiate from the tangential positions of Jung and Adler as from its more direct background in Freudian doctrine. This has been at-

2 The early foundations of Rank's views are sketched out in his *Truth and Reality*, especially Chapter I.

tempted in the foregoing chapters. In that connection many of Rank's views on personality were naturally touched upon briefly. It is, however, necessary at this point to bring his views together and to relate them in such a way as to reveal the unified pattern of Rank's personality theory.

Rank it must be noted, was not a systematic theorist and he was furthermore not at all interested in system building, such as preoccupied Freud during the later period. He therefore did not attempt to replace the Freudian system of personality theory but he sought rather to supplement, reformulate, revise, and eventually also to correct it at points of special interest to him as, in his view, this became increasingly necessary. This, in fact, was Rank's characteristic method of presenting his later views on most subjects, as will be indicated in a later connection.

In any event, insofar as the subject of personality is concerned, Rank does not present a systematic theory, corresponding in schematic detail to the Freudian. The view we get from his various works, although it is nowhere explicitly stated, is that we have many valuable insights into personality and its functioning in specific situations, in consequence of our experience with its expression in therapy, personal development and conduct, as well as in history and culture, but that we scarcely have a dependable basis for the formulation of such a schematized and universalized doctrine of personality structure and behavior, as is attempted by Freud in some of his later works. The shifting nature of Freud's own formulation from one work to another and, beyond Freud's own work, from one psychoanalytic writer to another, is itself clear evidence of this, according to him. In related areas of investigation, both psychological and cultural, there is, in Rank's view, equally striking and more comprehensive evidence that the Freudian goal of schematization and universalization of his doctrine, as represented by his later formulations, is essentially a misleading one. One must, from Rank's standpoint, allow for variability of temperament, disposition, background, and experience. Social change and cultural setting are factors of importance, as are also special interest and objective. In concrete detail, we thus necessarily have *psychologies,* not merely *psychology,* and personality *theories* not merely *theory.*[3]

Such was Rank's concession to the doctrine of psychological relativism, toward which, despite the contrary tendency of psychoanalysis, he appears always to have had a strong leaning on general philosophical grounds. In this leaning, he felt himself supported by recent developments and investigations, more particularly in the areas of world politics and cultural anthropology, the dramatic events and findings of which, unlike orthodox psychoanalysis, he accordingly had little difficulty in incorporating into his thinking.

With reference to the field of therapy, however, and personality as it is affected in the therapeutic situation, Rank's objections to the implications of Freudian schematization of theory had a more direct observational and experiential basis. For such schematization tends toward a formalization and routinization of the therapeutic process, according to him, toward what he has termed "ideological" therapy, which, as already noted, he considered obstructive of the real dynamic principle of the process, the free and creative interplay of relationship in the

[3] *Beyond Psychology,* Chaps. I, IV, VIII; *Truth and Reality,* Chaps. I, IV; *Modern Education,* Chaps. IV, V.

According to Rank, "Freud's tendency to absolutize his psychology was counteracted . . . by two diametrically opposed reactions: Adler's antithesis and Jung's synthesis, fulfilling, as it were, the dialectical completion of the whole system, thereby bringing the movement to a standstill."

Rank felt that the difference of emphasis in the personality theories of Freud, Jung, and Adler could well have been, in part, the result of the different types and classes of people with whom they were chiefly concerned. But in any event, he further explained: "That Freud's psychology, being an interpretation rather than an explanation of human nature, was not valid for all races, Jung pointed out; that it did not apply to different social environments, Adler emphasized; but that it did not even permit individuals of the same race and social background to deviate from the accepted type led me *beyond these differences in psychologies to a psychology of difference.*" (*Beyond Psychology,* p. 29.)

therapeutic situation. Against such a conception of therapy, therefore, Rank protested strenuously throughout the period of his differentiation of his position. Indeed, the bearing of Freudian doctrine on the practical conduct of the therapeutic process, having naturally been a central concern with Rank throughout the period of his differentiated psychotherapeutic activity, comment on this subject provided both the original occasion and the continuing incentive for the formulation of much of his distinctive theory, including his personality theory. Hence it is that the essentials of his distinctive position are so largely presented in terms of specific therapeutic problems and issues, the general import of which and application to other areas, being matters that frequently involve a difficult process of translation or even of basic reformulation. This has been the source of some of the differences of outlook and emphasis in the interpretation of Rankian doctrine which have come into evidence with the appearance of an increasing number of attempted applications of his views.[4]

With these introductory considerations in mind, the following points may be presented as essentials of Rank's position in its bearing on the subject of personality:

IMPULSE, INHIBITION, AND WILL

First and foremost, at any rate from the standpoint of its importance in defining his central theory, must be noted his increasing opposition to the overly passive and narrowly mechanistic psychoanalytic conception of personality and behavior in their relation to environment. At various times he expressed this opposition in different connections but in his later more distinctive formulations, his opposition was concentrated in an emphasis on "will" as the necessary corrective of the psychoanalytic picture. As already noted in connection with the preceding discussion of his therapeutic position, this concept, as

[4] See pp. 15-16; 83-86 and bibliography for specific references.

used by Rank, enabled him to present not only a more active
and flexible view of personality and behavior but also a more
positive, integrated, and especially more creative view. The importance of this concept in the whole framework of Rank's later
thinking, in fact, is so decisive and basic that it has increasingly
come into use to characterize his entire psychological outlook
and therapeutic procedure, as in the English translation of his
Technique of Psychoanalysis which appeared, with his approval,
under the title *Will Therapy*. This usage is unfortunate in one
respect, namely, that the status of the will concept in modern
psychology is such as to prejudice the unwary reader regarding
the implications of Rankian doctrine.[5] Furthermore, this emphasis appears to slight another important aspect of his theory
which is more concretely descriptive of his distinctive therapeutic position. Hence the alternative designation of his position
suggested in this work and elsewhere, likewise with Rank's

[5] It has already been suggested that Rank's formulations must be considered
in conjunction with his Freudian background which predominantly determined
both the content and form of his formulations. This point is discussed in greater
detail in Chap. VIII. As regards his emphasis on the will concept, this consideration has a special psychological, therapeutic, and social bearing. These connections have already been outlined and need not be repeated here, except to direct
special attention to the statements in reference to Rank's personality theory.
(See pp. 53-55; 58-60.)
    The schema of a constructive will psychology, in the center of which he places
the conscious ego, according to Rank, is as follows: Instinct lifted into the ego
sphere by consciousness is the power of will, and at the same time a tamed,
directed, controlled instinct, which manifests itself freely within the individual
personality, that is creatively. Just as the creative will represents the conscious
expression of instinct, so emotion represents the conscious awareness of instinct.
In both cases, it is consciousness which lends to the phenomenon its authentic
psychological significance.
    The influence of the power of consciousness on the ego-ideal formation has a
double effect likewise, an active and a passive one; active in the creative expression of the ego-ideal, passive in the formation of definite ethical, aesthetic, and
logical norms, without whose concurrence no kind of action is possible. These
norms modify still further the content of the instinctual drives, which were
already modified by consciousness, since they prescribe the only possible form in
which the individual can realize and objectify his instinctual drives. In these
terms, Rank restates the Freudian concepts of id, ego, and super-ego and leads
to what he describes as "a philosophy of the psychic," developed in his *Truth
and Reality*. (*Truth and Reality*, pp. 48-9; *Beyond Psychology*, p. 50.)

approval. Additional consideration of this matter will appear in connection with later comment on the concept of "relationship."

Of similar but more limited import is his presentation of "inhibition" as a basic and increasingly autonomous internal process rather than a secondary and externally imposed factor in behavior, as it is presented in the orthodox Freudian doctrine of repression. This point again has special historical significance in that it links up with Rank's novel theory of anxiety and fear as developed in his *Trauma of Birth*, the publication of which, as has been noted in several previous connections, marked the public severance of his close professional association with Freud. In an historical sense, in fact, Rank's theory of inhibition represented his first important line of deviation from Freudian thought and hence it is historically related, both directly and indirectly in terms of the above-mentioned special theories, to many of the distinctive features of his position.[6]

On a more conscious level, inhibition takes on the form of "denial," conceived of by him as the more constructive and creative therapeutic equivalent of the psychoanalytic doctrine of repression. The important consideration in respect to both inhibition and denial is that they are viewed by Rank as negative will expressions and hence, as in the case of resistance, they may be therapeutically transformed into positive will expression.[7] As such, they are no longer regarded as Freudian entities

6 Rank noted in a special comment, by way of indicating the historical importance of his view of inhibition in the crystallization of his position, that his conception actually dates back to his pre-Freudian era as represented by his early work, *Der Künstler*, completed in 1905 before he came directly under the influence of Freud. In his *Truth and Reality*, especially Chapter I, this early background of his doctrine is indicated and related to various other aspects of his theory; also *Art and Artist*, pp. 39-41, 46; *Beyond Psychology*, pp. 274-76, 282-83.

7 "The key to these phenomena," says Rank, "is found in will psychology. For at bottom we deal always with denial of willing," which itself is originally negative in character, a "not wanting to," as when the child begins to resist and says "I won't." But as already stated, it is the function of will therapy to change these negative forms of will expression into positive forms. "The goal of constructive therapy," he says, "is the transformation of the negative will expression . . . .

but as functions of the unifying concept of will which, in all its varied transformations, as Rank repeatedly stated, accordingly becomes the essential psychological problem for him.[8]

"Impulse" is similarly viewed by Rank as the dynamic aspect of will and as such represents an implied and often directed criticism of the Freudian biologically oriented instinct conception of personality and behavior. This change of conception is reflected in Rank's increasing use of the neutral term impulse, and correspondingly in his more reserved and conditional use of the term instinct. With Rank, as with other writers, the term impulse, when deliberately employed by him, appears to cut across the orthodox distinction between instinctive drive and social conditioning, thus allowing for a more unified view of innate and acquired factors in the structure of personality and as determinants of behavior.

Like Jung, Rank gradually came to recognize other basic drives than the sexual, particularly the constantly emphasized "creative impulse" which, in its essential implications, would seem to stand in direct contrast to the notion of instinctive patterning, as well as to the Freudian view of the sexual character of its content. In the elaboration of his will doctrine, this impulse and the associated "creative will principle" gradually came to have central importance in Rank's thought, just as the spiritual libido tendency observed by Jung, similarly came to have central importance in Jung's system of thought. In each case, this was the result of developing convictions about personality and behavior, which ultimately brought these positions

---

into positive and eventually creative expression." (*Will Therapy*, pp. 28, 45-6; *Art and Artist*, pp. 39-40.)

8 He states: "The essential problem of psychology is our abolition of the fact of will, the explanation of the manifold types of abolition of will and its varying interpretation at different times. This psychological problem, actually *the* problem of psychology, as it meets us in psychoanalysis, is therefore a universal problem" and will becomes the central problem of personality and psychology. (*Will Therapy*, pp. 15-16, 45-6; *Art and Artist*, pp. 9, 28.)

into inevitable conflict with the narrower and more specialized biological emphasis of Freudian doctrine.[9]

CONSCIOUSNESS, THE UNCONSCIOUS, AND PSYCHOSEXUALITY

Consistent with Rank's broader and more integrative outlook, as represented by the foregoing triad of basic points of interpretation, is his increasing tendency to disregard the orthodox antithesis between conscious and unconscious motivation, both as a theoretical distinction and a therapeutic device.[10] Likewise consistent with this viewpoint, is his clear tendency to subdue the predominance of the psychoanalytic doctrine of psychosexuality and, along with it, the one-sided sexual interpretation of the whole range of psychoanalytic phenomena and related material.[11] While Rank never dissociated himself from Freudian thought in the dramatic manner of Jung and Adler, he thus redefined his position in as fundamental, if not more fundamental, terms. This has long been recognized in the field of therapy but on the theoretical side, his position has failed to receive corresponding attention, due, no doubt, to the inaccessibility, until recent years, of much of his pertinent technical material and the special difficulties associated with the reformu-

9 Though at times separately considered, impulse and inhibition are really aspects, according to Rank, of the unifying concept of will and thus are most frequently referred to in terms of will in the elaboration of his will psychology. (*Art and Artist,* p. 39.)

10 As soon as we restore to the will its psychological rights, according to Rank, the "psychology of the unconscious" unveils itself as one of the numerous attempts to deny the will "in order to evade the conscious responsibility following of necessity therefrom." The unavoidable guilt feeling resulting shows the failure of the attempt; it "is as it were the 'neurotic' throw-back of the denied responsibility." (*Truth and Reality,* pp. 50-1.)

11 It will be recalled that Rank defined will as "a positive guiding organization and integration of self which utilizes creatively, as well as inhibits and controls the instinctual drives." (See p. 53.) This applies to the sexual impulse, particularly. Animals may be *driven* by their appetites, but the distinctive feature about man is that he can control, direct, and creatively transform them, according to Rank; in the case of sexuality especially by love, which lifts its expression from the biological level merely to the complex human and cultural level. (*Will Therapy,* p. 79 ff.; *Truth and Reality,* chap. V; *Beyond Psychology,* chap. V.)

lation of his technical discussions in more general terms, as already previously indicated.

In line with the latter statement, it may be observed that even some of the foregoing points represent a superstructure of generalization from more specific therapeutic formulations dealing with such problems and issues as were outlined in the previous chapter. This is merely noted in this connection by way of referring again to the primary therapeutic foundation of Rank's more generalized views and theories. Such reference to the technical basis of his position is the more necessary because most previous summaries and discussions of Rankian thought have concentrated on this underlying therapeutic aspect of his position, to the almost complete neglect of its broader theoretical implications and considerations. Thus the distinctive features of Rank's technical deviations are much more widely familiar to students of psychotherapy than his more general theoretical formulations.

RELATIONSHIP

In his *Will Therapy* and some of his other later formulations, Rank brought the general therapeutic concept of "relationship" into view as a determining consideration, alike in therapy and in personal development more generally. Here we accordingly have another concept of basic importance in Rank's distinctively formulated position, so that, as has already been indicated in various connections, "relationship" and "will" have become identifying characteristics of Rank's views.[12] While relationship is not as frequently stressed explicitly, it is neverthe-

---

[12] It has already been noted (p. 59) that will and relationship represent, among other important features of his distinctive theory, Rank's original approach to the reinterpretation of the basic psychoanalytic concepts of resistance and transference, the distinguishing premises, according to Freud, of psychoanalytic therapy. It is understandable, therefore, that will and relationship should occupy a position of central importance in Rank's theory, just as resistance and transference similarly occupy a position of central importance in psychoanalytic theory.

less foundational in Rank's thinking both historically and therapeutically, since it is intimately linked with his central theory in *The Trauma of Birth* and is featured as the underlying therapeutic conception of his *Will Therapy*, the subtitle of which reads, as has been noted, "An Analysis of the Therapeutic Process in Terms of Relationship." It thus provides, in a purely psychological and therapeutic sense, not only the essential setting for the consideration of specific therapeutic problems such, for example, as separation and termination, but it also establishes the interactional atmosphere of Rank's more general personality and cultural theory.

In any event, it is safe to conclude that "relationship" and "will" constitute two points of fundamental emphasis in Rankian thought which are of primary importance in characterizing his position. They represent complementary and not conflicting points of emphasis, so that it is particularly significant to consider them in connection with each other. Also, Rank's willingness to accept either or both as a characterization of his distinctive orientation is consistent with his general opposition to narrow or one-sided categorization of his position. This is a consideration of importance in interpreting all attempts to epitomize his doctrine.

An important special aspect of relationship which was considered in connection with Rank's therapy is "separation." The manner in which Rank applies these two concepts to the interpretation of the relational aspects of personality development is an impressive feature of his personality theory. Human development proceeds, according to him, in terms of relationship and separation by a succession of emotional attachments and dependencies on the one hand and independence-seeking separations and detachments on the other hand, with the creation of personality and the emergence of individuality as constantly evolving and expanding goals. From the primal attachment and separation at birth to the final detachment and separation at death, this process of binding and freeing continues, throughout the entire course of human life. It constitutes the "dialectic" of human growth and development on the relational or interpersonal plane. The elemental importance of the process and its many-sided reference to human psychology and therapy, indicate the significance of the concepts of relationship and separation in Rank's personality theory. "Life Fear and Death Fear" and "Total Ego and Partial Ego" are closely associated aspects of this process which Rank develops in their therapeutic connections, while "The Birth of Individuality," "The Creation of Personality," and "The Emergence of the Social Self" are similarly associated aspects which he develops in terms of personality theory and the socio-cultural setting of the process.[13]

Unlike the will concept which Rank took over as an organizing concept from the fields of psychology and philosophy after he became sensitized to the therapeutic manifestations of will phenomena, he arrived at the relationship concept directly from his therapeutic observation and experience and his consequent attempt to reinterpret the psychoanalytic conception of transference in terms of mother-centered dependency. This fundamental shift of focus, as has already been noted in several specific connections, resulted in major theoretical as well as therapeutic changes and gradually assumed a predominent importance in defining Rank's distinctive conception of the therapeutic process. At any rate, relationship is firmly anchored empirically in his experience with therapy, despite its intimate association with his early theoretical formulation of the trauma of birth doctrine. In his later formulations, relationship is developed by Rank on the purely psychological and social planes and thus is merged with his will psychology.[14]

13 *Will Therapy*, Book I, chap. VII and Book II, chaps. II, III; *Truth and Reality*, chaps. I, V; *Beyond Psychology*, chaps. III, IV, VIII.

14 On whatever plane relationship occurs, it naturally assumes a participating "other," whether it be the mother, the family, or the larger community, through whom a participating experience, which is its special characteristic, may be achieved. As so frequently, Rank develops this theme culturally and historically. In earlier times, according to him, man achieved uniting communal expe-

RELATIONSHIP AND THE SOCIO-CULTURAL PERSPECTIVE

Taken in conjunction with the social-cultural perspective of Rank's thought generally, the indicated relationship view of the specific phenomena and processes of interaction which concretize it in therapy and personal development, tends to bring Rankian thought notably into line with the direction of development represented by modern social psychology. The latter has similarly been marked by an emphasis on relationship in tracing out the functional interrelation of the individual and the social-cultural factors in personality and behavior.[15] This point thus brings to a head the essential difference of focus which characterizes Rankian as compared with Freudian thought and at the same time suggests the broadened psychosocial implications and possibilities of the Rankian position. These, however, regrettably remain only scantily developed in Rank's works, insofar as systematic presentation is concerned,

---

rience" by participation of group members in rituals of renewal. "Such experience was more deeply rooted than our psychological 'identification,' which is but a faint individualistic echo of a uniting communal experience." In our individualistic life, "the personality's constant need for support and justification" depends on substitute types of participation. This is the function specifically performed by therapy and more generally by other kinds of participation which, however, may not fully replace "the collective security of the group" in less individualistic patterns of life. The price which all have to pay in our modern world "for this personal independence from the group is another kind of *individual* dependence which we call relationship." Paradoxically, the individualistic person tends more toward the development of relationship and not toward aloneness, as might be supposed. "On this plane of individualistic relationship, personality is shaped and formed according to the vital need to please the other person whom we make our 'God' . . . The neurotic and the criminal type only represent outstanding examples of such failure in individual relationship, as our modern basis of personality development." (*Beyond Psychology*, pp. 165-69.)

15 The chief aspects of this development, culminating in modern social psychology as it has come to be known in this country, have been traced out by the author in *American Social Psychology*, which thus presents various points of significant comparison with Rankian thought in respect to its social-psychological implications. A more recent analysis appears in the writer's article entitled "American Social Psychology—1951," *American Journal of Sociology*, Vol. XVIII (Sept. 1952) , pp. 187-193.

even though his later interest led increasingly toward elaboration along these lines.[16]

In his *Will Therapy, Modern Education,* and especially in his *Art and Artist,* nevertheless, these implications and possibilities are more specifically developed and thus we see that, whereas Rank primarily continued the pattern and interest of Freudian thought, he passed far beyond the limitations of his original background and opened up possibilities of harmonious integration with related areas of thought and investigation, such as few positions associated with psychoanalysis present. In fact, it is not until we come to the recent work in the same direction by such present-day reinterpreters of Freud as, for example, Karen Horney in some of her later reformulations of Freudian doctrine, that we get a similar integrative approach to personality and behavior in relation to the social-cultural environment developed from the psychoanalytic standpoint.[17]

PERSONALITY TYPES

In connection with his more general personality doctrine as outlined, Rank has identified three special personality types as over against the average, more or less well adjusted normal personality: the artist or creative type, the neurotic type, and the anti-social (criminal and psychopathic) type. These he related to the triad, will-inhibition-impulse as organizing principles, so that, according to him, will is predominant as an organizing principle in the case of the creative type, inhibition in the case of the neurotic type, and impulse in the case of the anti-social type. From this standpoint, all of these special types are marked

[16] Rank's posthumously published volume, *Beyond Psychology* (1941), was actually presented as an attempt to outline certain aspects of his conception of social psychology, but the conception is not developed systematically enough and is not sufficiently related to his previous works to do justice to the fundamental pattern of his previous thought.

[17] Independently produced and reflecting a distinct orientation and a more direct connection with American sociological and anthropological thought, Karen Horney's *The Neurotic Personality of Our Time* (1937) and *New Ways in Psychoanalysis* (1939) have many basic points in common with Rank's views.

by an imbalance or one-sidedness in development. If the slant is sufficient to establish itself as the determining principle of the personality, we have clear-cut types, or, if less decided, a predominance merely of mood and attitude. The average, so-called normal personality is, by comparison with these special types, better balanced and more harmoniously integrated but, at the same time, less productive creatively.

This being a social and therapeutic as well as psychological classification, it is of importance to recall that Rank relates the neurotic to the artist type, rather than to the normal personality, as is the more frequent practice. The neurotic, according to him, is the artistic temperament that miscarries and fails to achieve artistic expression. Hence the neurotic represents a failure in creativity essentially rather than a failure in normal development. This conception sets the primary therapeutic problem of the neurotic from Rank's standpoint and suggests the basis for much that is distinctive in his view of therapy as regards the handling of the neurotic type, particularly his emphasis on creative expression in the therapeutic situation as the core of the therapeutic process.

It has already been mentioned that Rank as well as Jung, objected especially to the psychoanalytic conception of artistic expression in terms of sublimation. It was Rank's increasing disagreement with this conception which originally led him to attempt a classification of personality types in order to differentiate between the neurotic and the creative types. The need for such differentiation, psychoanalysis of course failed to recognize because of its one-sided generalizing interest which, as Rank frequently pointed out, is nevertheless based upon observation only of the neurotic type. On the basis of his own observations, he gradually came to feel that in this respect, in the attempt to distinguish personality types, Jung complimented Freud in a very necessary direction. While his own classification differs from Jung's, it incorporates a similar principle of psychological and psychotherapeutic differentiation.

Beyond this direct psychological and psychotherapeutic

angle, furthermore, the effect of Rank's detailed analysis of the artist and neurotic types, in describing the relation of personality and social setting, is to bring more concretely into view the social-cultural orientation and import of his general framework of interpretation as already outlined. Rarely in analytic doctrine, is the functional interrelation of individual and social elements so suggestively presented in reference to the concrete give-and-take of relationship in the therapeutic situation on the one hand and of interacton in the larger social-cultural situation on the other. Rank's conception reflects an altogether special significance to his analysis of these two types in their complementary relation to each other and in the complementary interplay of mood and attitude in behavior more generally, alike in therapy and in the wider processes of social life.[18]

PERSONALITY AND INDIVIDUATION

The broadened social reference and perspective noted in the last two sections must be viewed in the case of Rank, as was previously stated, in relation to his constant and characteristic emphasis on the unique and individual aspects of behavior and personality, which we get as a part of his theory of will and creativity. This reciprocal individualized viewpoint is stressed alike in its constructive and negative aspects in various connections touching upon the characteristic features of his position and is presented with particular effect in his analysis of the creative and neurotic types in their respective functioning in the therapeutic and art processes.

As was noted in the section on relationship, the process of individualization is an aspect of the dialectic of human growth and development which was described in terms of relationship and separation as continuing throughout the course of human life. "The never completed birth of individuality" has to do, according to Rank, "with a conflictual separation of the indi-

18 *Art and Artist,* pp. 40-41.

vidual from the mass, undertaken and continued at every step of development into the new." It is beset by fears of isolation and the loss of hard-won physical, psychological, and social securities. On this account, Rank viewed the process in terms of birth symbolism, as somehow corresponding to the biological process "of procreation and birth."

He described its course of development as follows: "The whole consequence of evolution from blind impulse through conscious will to self conscious knowledge, seem still somehow to correspond to a continued result of births, rebirths and new births, which reach from the birth of the child from the mother, beyond the birth of the individual from the mass, to the birth of the creative work from the individual and finally to the birth of knowledge from the work." We find in all these phenomena, even at the highest spiritual peak, according to him, "the struggle and pain of birth, the separation out of the universal . . . the creation of an own individual cosmos, whether it be now physically our own child, creatively our own work or spiritually our own self."[19]

Like the interpenetrating and simultaneously developing aspects of the process, The Creation of Personality and The Emergence of the Social Self, individualization is at bottom, as Rank states, a process of self-creative will expression and thus is an integral part of his will psychology.

It is clear, therefore, that Rank's viewpoint is in this respect also integrative, that is, it is never one-sided but rests squarely, as he frequently maintained, "on two legs": the generalizing and individualizng, the personal and the social, the individual and the collective. This integrated two-sided approach was historically one of his distinctive contributions to analytic doctrine and it has continued throughout to be a notable and characteristic feature of his position.[20] In consequence of this outlook,

19 *Truth and Reality*, pp. 24-25.
20 Some of Rank's own specific statements on the importance of this integrative approach, which he himself has termed "social-psychological," are of interest, in

Rank may be said to be primarily concerned not with the biological individual of classical psychoanalysis, who is dramatically in conflict with his social world, but rather with "the-individual-in-relation" to his conditioning social-cultural environment, and increasingly, with both the-individual-in-relation and the social-cultural environment in active and reciprocal interaction with each other. This is a point of basic significance and many-sided implications for both theory and therapy, some of which have recently been impressively developed by Karen Horney and others of the neo-Freudian group who have been especially engaged in harmonizing psychoanalytic doctrine with the findings of modern social-cultural studies.

SELF-DETERMINATION AND ACTIVE ADJUSTMENT

By way of summary, it may be re-emphasized that in reference to the subject of personality, the effect of Rank's position as outlined, has been to replace the atomistic, antithetical, passive, and deterministic view of behavior and personality, which follows from the psychoanalytic conception of primary instinctive drives and derived social repressions, with a more synthetic, unified, self-assertive, and creative view. In broader social terms, his position leads to a view of active self-expression and control of adjustment and environment, as against the more passive psychoanalytic doctrine of blind force, in the form of primary instinct patterns as the chief determinants of individual adaptation to external reality. The latter point is notable in that passivity, both as a technical device and a social principle, has at times been attributed to Rank, though in both connections, it is basically inconsistent with his characteristic position, as must be evident from the repeated emphasis on the

---

view of renewed activity in this direction by psychoanalytic writers who, like Rank, have recently come under the influence of the social-cultural perspective. See, for example, *Art and Artist*, pp. xiv, xviii, 25-6; 396-97.

contrary conception. That such an interpretation of his position should be possible under the circumstances, despite individual statements that might be quoted out of context, is accordingly challenging and would seem to require some comment.

In large part, the situation is explainable by the fact that Rankian thought, because of its peculiar history and conditions of development, as previously sketched, reflects various stages of differentiation from Freudian doctrine and correspondingly, various conflicting elements, if viewed as a unit rather than by periods of development. From this complex of doctrine, the reader often chooses inevitably, in accordance with his own interest, outlook, and critical standpoint. This has had its advantages historically as well as its disadvantages, but it has at times definitely contributed to confusion. On the above point, so close to the central theme of Rankian thought, however, there would be little room for difference of opinion, were it uncomplicated by external considerations. For on the technical side, the question of activity and passivity, as already described, was one of the earliest points of controversy leading to the differentiation of Rankian procedure.[21] And on the theoretical side, Rank had long termed Freudian doctrine "a philosophy of despair" and his increasing emphasis on will was, in part, an attempt to offset the passive psychoanalytic viewpoint. His position in this regard has already been summarized in the previous chapter. In view of the approved form of this statement, reference is made to it in this connection.[22]

[21] Rank had commented on Ferenczi's active procedures by stating that "all therapy, by nature, is 'active,' that is it purposes an effect through volitional influence and a change resulting from it." The passivity of psychoanalysis; according to him, is a virtue in the investigator not in the therapist, who "must proceed 'actively' . . . if he aims at attaining any therapeutic effect worthy of the name." He then explained that the reason that psychoanalysis has failed to recognize this is that in the classical analytic situation "the person of the therapist stood in the center," so that the patient must adjust to the therapist rather than the other way around, when "the patient himself as the chief actor" is placed in the center of the therapeutic situation and his reactions are utilized constructively as opportunities for assistance in the strengthening of his personality. (*The Trauma of Birth*, p. 203; *Will Therapy*, pp. 9-10, 21.)

[22] See pp. 54-55.

Because of the larger social implications of his position, in fact, the Rankian viewpoint has appeared more consistent with the American cultural background than it otherwise would, and Rank has accordingly had, from the first, a special vogue in this country, despite the unfamiliar character of some of his specific doctrines.

APPLICATIONS AND AN ILLUSTRATION

In view of the broadened psychological, therapeutic, and social reference of Rankian theory, it is natural that his views should have a many-sided appeal to those who, for various reasons, find themselves critical of the limitations of psychoanalytic doctrine, not only in the fields of therapy, art, and education, in which Rank's own major efforts were concentrated, but also in new areas, such as counseling, guidance, and social work, in which his own work, in accordance with his essential position, can serve only as a suggestive basis for detailed elaboration in the distinctive terms of these particular areas of application. This matter, insofar as social work in particular is concerned, requires more detailed consideration, in consequence of Rank's special and significant association with this field, as was noted at the end of the preceding chapter.

It is necessary to recall, therefore, by way of illustration in this particular connection, that in the field of social work, as in other areas, the introduction of Rankian thought on a previous background of unchallenged Freudian influence has naturally precipitated some defensive controversy. Like other representatives of deviating positions from psychoanalysis, Rank has thus at times been subjected to unfavorable criticism by Freudian oriented practitioners on various grounds, but particularly on the ground that he is not sufficiently "scientific" in his essential viewpoint and emphasis. Since, however, this charge has been levelled also against all other analytic positions, including the Freudian, it is of no special concern in respect to Rankian doctrine, except as it indicates the uncertain state of psychotherapeutic doctrine generally at the present time, and the common need of a process of dependable verification in this entire area, in selecting out the valid from the questionable elements. Until such validation is achieved, it is inevitable that preference for one or another position will be determined by external and accidental considerations rather than on the basis of an objective appraisal of the actual merits of the several positions. And as always in such cases, justifications will be sought on what are essentially irrelevant grounds because, in the absence of reliable criteria, no generally acceptable justification is at hand.[23]

Returning, then, to the more direct consideration of the relation of Rankian thought to social work, it is pertinent to inquire what, as a matter of historical record, has been Rank's influence on social work? As in other areas, it has already been stated, Rankian thought was introduced into the field of social work on a background of Freudian doctrine and hence Rankian thought served, in the first place, as a ferment to keep discussion and experimentation in this area active and thus to prevent an uncritical adherence to a single viewpoint and technical procedure. For several years preceding, and more conspicuously since the publication of *A Changing Psychology in Social Case Work* (1930) by Virginia Robinson and *The Dynamics of Therapy in a Controlled Relationship* (1933) by Jessie Taft, Rankian thought has also been a prominant center of positive influence in the field, both directly through Rank's own works and teaching connections, and indirectly through the challenging applications of his viewpoint which have been made in the analysis of social work situations and processes.[24] During this period,

[23] As a matter of fact, Rank never claimed scientific validity for his views; only a critical appraisal of the available evidence, in which respect, he felt, Freudian thought was particularly lacking. Furthermore, he did not believe that therapy should or could be scientific in the narrow sense of Freudian thought. According to him, Freud himself was primarily a philosopher in the later formulation of his views but his followers refused to admit it and to be governed accordingly. If they had admitted it, he felt, they would have saved the movement much bitter controversy and opposition. (*Beyond Psychology*, pp. 47, 277-78.)

[24] Especially to be noted as a source of supplementary influence in the social

the field has been kept much more tolerantly experimental and constructively critical than it would otherwise have been, insofar as psychoanalysis is concerned, largely as a result of the competing influence of Rank's views. It is not too much to say that some of the most significant developments in the therapeutic aspects of social work during this period have been defined by interests rooted, in the first place, in his thought-provoking and suggestive formulation of therapeutic doctrine.

Insofar as social work is concerned, Rank has been exceptionally fortunate in the type of following he attracted, especially during the first period of popularization of his position. As is easily understandable from the nature of his basic points of emphasis, his position has appealed to the more imaginative and resourceful representatives of the field who have been willing and able to contribute constructively to the elaboration of his views. This has kept his position alert and adaptable to the developing needs of the field. It has also introduced elements of conflicting interpretation, as already previously noted, because of differences of interest and outlook. But this, in itself, has become a challenge toward further clarification and may have its positive aspects at a time when our information about the fundamental matters involved is still so limited, shifting, and controversial. In any event, Rank adopted as a guide in this respect, the goal envisaged in the quotation from Kant which he gives in his *Will Therapy:*

"You will learn from me not philosophy but to philosophize, not thoughts to be imitated but to think."

This was his attitude in reference to applications of his views in the field of social work, as in other areas. It is an attitude which has definite hazards but these, he regarded less serious to

work field is the series of publications put out by the Pennsylvania School of Social Work of the University of Pennsylvania dealing with various areas of application and, under their sponsorship, the continued popularization and translation of Rank's works.

his viewpoint than inflexibility of application of any position, including his own.

It is of course not uncommon for analysts to be associated with the field of social work, for this field has long been one of the chief consumers of their services. But Rank's association was distinctive in that social work served as a medium for the development and interpretation of his views, which the more individualistically oriented field of private analytic practice, defined, as it has been, by the orthodox psychoanalytic approach, failed to provide. Furthermore, the field of social work, as has been indicated, also served as a center for the dissemination of his views and for the extension of his influence into various other areas, so that his position is today secure despite all opposition on the part of more orthodox groups.

It is disconcerting to some Freudians that anyone should prefer Adler or Jung or Rank to Freud and the fact that this is so is a challenge to the predominant influence of the Freudian group. But at present this early group of deviant analytic therapists is expanded by more recent nonconformist groups, neo-Freudian and others. And this bodes well for the clarification of important issues which are of common interest to all of the analytic groups and to the varied fields of related therapeutic, counseling, and social work practice as well.

Chapter VII

OEDIPUS COMPLEX AND BIRTH TRAUMA

In the Preface to the *Trauma of Birth,* Rank states that "whoever is familiar with the course of psychoanalytic investigation, will not be astonished to find that this method ultimately reaches a point at which it finds its natural limitation, but likewise also its foundation." He proceeds to explain that after a thorough examination of the unconscious, "we have come up against the final origin of the psychical unconscious in the psycho-physical, which we can now make biologically comprehensible as well." Elaborating on this underlying thought further, he says:

"In attempting to reconstruct for the first time from analytic experiences the to all appearances purely physical birth trauma with its prodigious psychical consequences for the whole development of mankind, we are led to recognize in the birth trauma the ultimate biological basis of the phychical. In this way we gain a fundamental insight into the nucleus of the Unconscious on which Freud has constructed which may claim to be comprehensive and scientific. In this sense, the following arguments are only possible and intelligible on the basis of the whole body of knowledge gained psychoanalitically, about the construction and the functioning of our own phychical instrument."[1]

[1] *Trauma of Birth,* p. xiii.

This is the core of Rank's controversial thesis, the impressive development of which constitutes the volume here under consideration. Rank brought to bear his highly developed cultural approach to the many-sided elaboration and illustration of this thesis so that, in effect, the volume took on the proportions of a psychoanalytic culture history or, as Rank termed it, a "history of the development of the human mind and of the things created by it." The volume thus represents one of the most comprehensive attempts to extend psychoanalytic thought along culture-historical lines. It certainly represents the high-point of Rank's constructive attempt in this direction, and the extent of the effort which he lavished on the preparation of this work may be taken as a measure of the importance which he attached to its underlying thesis, as indicated above.

One can easily imagine, also, how difficult it must have been for Freud, under the circumstances and in view of his own developing interest in the cultural extension of psychoanalytic doctrine, to be obliged, in the course of events as already described, to dissociate himself from this impressive formulation, especially after the positive manner in which Rank linked the volume to its psychoanalytic foundations. For Rank not only tells us that the volume represents a first attempt to apply the psychoanalytic way of thinking "to the comprehension of the whole development of mankind," but the contents of the volume actually constitute an attempt to translate the claim into concrete psychoanalytic terms and subject-matter.

In spite of the fact that so much controversy has centered about this volume, it presents a definitely Freudian orientation and, as stated, is throughout positively linked to its Freudian background. The very conception of the "birth trauma" as well as the suggestion regarding its importance in human psychology are Freud's. For example, in his lecture on "Fear and Anxiety" Freud says:

"We believe we know the early impression which the

emotion of fear repeats. We think it is birth itself which combines that complex of painful feelings, of a discharge of impulses, of physical sensations, which has become the prototype for the effect of danger to life, and is ever after repeated within us as a condition of fear. . . . The name anxiety—angustial—narrowness, emphasizes the characteristic tightening of the breath, which was at the time a consequence of an actual situation and is henceforth repeated almost regularly in the emotion. We shall also recognize how significant it is that this first condition of fear appeared during the first separation from the mother. Of course, we are convinced that the tendency to repetition of the first condition of fear has been so deeply ingrained in the organism through countless generations, that not a single individual can escape the emotion of fear; not even the mythical Macduff . . . . who did not experience birth itself."[2]

Rank became increasingly convinced of the importance of this conception on the basis of his own analytic work and his cultural studies, and it was certainly his original intention to follow out Freud's lead constructively, from a psychoanalytic standpoint.[3] But the opposition which his attempt at elaboration of the conception met, led him to begin to take basic stock of the whole situation, with the result that, as he later tells us, his *Trauma of Birth* actually became the turning point of his thought and career.

Why did Freud disregard this thesis after having attributed such importance to it? Rank began to wonder. And why was there so much opposition to his elaboration of some of the implications of the conception, even though the elaboration was definitely made in the spirit of Freudian thought and analytic evidence? Rank felt that there must be some deep under-

[2] *A General Introduction to Psycho-analysis*, p. 345; also *New Introductory Lectures on Psycho-analysis*, pp. 119-22.

[3] "We would like to regard our arguments concerning the importance of the trauma of birth for Psychoanalysis," Rank tells us in this work, "only as a contribution to the Freudian structure of normal psychology, at best as one of its pillars." (*Trauma of Birth*, p. 210.)

lying reason which would provide the answers to these questions. And gradually plausible answers began to appear. Could it be that this conception which places the mother relationship at the center of psychoanalytic doctrine threatened the patriarchal structure of Freudian thought? For in the Freudian system, as Rank later noted, the father is made "into a figure of God-like power" and the masculine principle is not only predominant, but man is made the measure against whom woman is appraised, with the result that she is interpreted only in terms of negative characteristics.[4]

Rank's comparative cultural approach taught him to see this as a cultural limitation, and especially in the biological form of psychoanalytic doctrine, also as a reversal of the natural order. Furthermore, he became increasingly convinced that it led to a misinterpretation of important therapeutic evidence. But he also realized how futile it was to struggle against such deeply-based opposition, and so he finally determined to go his own way, just as Freud himself had done when he found himself in opposition to conventional thought. The consequences of this determination on the part of Rank have already been outlined.

In this particular connection, the result was that what began as only an attempt to establish psychoanalytic thought on a still deeper foundation than the Oedipus level,[5] eventually became, in the course of Rank's later thinking, a fundamental change of theoretical orientation as well as therapeutic perspective. It is in this latter sense that Rank's "trauma of birth" conception has been looked upon as being inconsistent with the dominant role of the "Oedipus complex" in Freudian thought and, in fact, as a rival theory, especially as later reinterpreted by Rank.

For, as he gradually freed himself from the Freudian biological pattern of thought, Rank abandoned his original attempt, following the Freudian pattern, to establish his theory biologically. He directed himself increasingly, rather, to the

---

4 *Beyond Psychology*, p. 275.
5 *Trauma of Birth*, pp. 21-2, 194, 216.

psychological, symbolic, and cultural interpretation of the mother-child relationship as not only the basic human relationship but also the dominant relationship pattern in all of human life. It is in this frame of reference that his consideration of such concepts, among others, as "anxiety," "fear," "relationship," "ending," and "separation" in therapy, take on a special significance.

Whatever may be said for and against Rank's trauma of birth theory, there is an appealing element of poetic justice about it as a balance against the one-sided masculine-centered Freudian system of thought. This is a corrective balance which periodically reappears in biological, psychological, and social thought; recently, for example, in Margaret Mead's *Male and Female,* as well as in the more direct analytic criticisms of Karen Horney, Clara Thompson, and others, as well as Rank.[6] All of this indicates how culture-limited our theories of personality and human behavior still are or, as Rank maintained, how relativistic our knowledge of these phenomena continues to be, despite all our claims to scientific objectivity and our elaborate research procedures.

The Freudian masculine-centered system of psychology naturally comes to a focus in the discussion of "the psychology of women" which, as already suggested, has been severely criticized on various grounds. There is little doubt that this is one of the weakest and culturally insensitive aspects of Freudian thought. It recalls early nineteenth century child and ethnic psychology, which likewise were negatively developed in terms of "lacks" and "inferiorities" and not "altogether flattering" observations, on the basis of a comparison with nineteenth century European adult psychology, which was accepted as the standard of all psychology, the standard, however, varying with the particular nationality of the psychologist making the comparison. Freud

[6] Horney, *New Ways in Psychoanalysis,* chap. VI; Thompson, *Psychoanalysis, Evolution and Development,* chap. VII; Rank, *Beyond Psychology,* chaps. VII, VIII.

himself mentions the possibility of his being accused of having an *idée fixe* on the subject and this is a manifestly applicable description of his position.[7]

According to Rank, it was only very gradually and very late in his career, that Freud was induced to separate the development of the girl from that of the boy and to moderate somewhat his "derogatory attitude" toward and his "ego-centric" conception of the psychology of women in terms of a "no-man" or an emasculated male. His reluctance to do so, according to Rank, was only overcome "by theoretical disagreement with some of his followers, especially women,[8] and can be understood from the fact that such an admission of difference would invalidate his fundamental conception, the Oedipus-complex." Reluctantly, and for that matter purely theoretically, Rank states, "did Freud assign to his all-important father-figure the second place and acknowledge the predominant role of the mother for the girl's development."[9]

Basically, however, according to Rank, Freud's conception of woman "is not of an independent individual in her own right but as an instrument of man's procreative ideology." It is a conception which could only be advanced, Rank held, from the standpoint of "masculine inferiority which is rooted in man's fear of woman" and this "inferiority complex" Freud projected unto woman "in order to save the crumbling ideology" of his father-ideal. "This gigantic projection," says Rank, "was naturally bound to fail" and it did fail through the deviant inter-

---

[7] *New Introductory Lectures on Psycho-analysis*, p. 181.

[8] Rank had reference particularly to the critical culturally oriented approach to the psychology of women as well as to psychoanalytic subject-matter more generally represented by the work of Karen Horney (*New Ways in Psychoanalysis*, 1939, chaps. VI, X.) in contrast to the much more conservative psychoanalytic standpoint represented, for example, by the work of Helene Deutsch (*The Psychology of Women*, two volumes, 1944, 1945). A middle-of-the-road position characteristic of the Washington school is represented more recently by Clara Thompson (*Psychoanalysis, Evolution and Development*, 1950, Preface and chap. VII).

[9] *Beyond Psychology*, p. 286.

pretations presented, in the first place, by Adler and Jung, followed by his own differentiated position, and thereafter by various others, including especially women analysts, as noted.[10]

The contrasting argument to the Freudian, is bluntly stated from the cultural standpoint by Margaret Mead in terms of "womb-envy" and runs somewhat as follows: Men cannot have babies! Boys gradually learn this conspicuous and impressive fact and gradually assimilate "the shock," and men adapt to and seek compensation for this "basic inferiority" through effort and struggle and through various types of cultural arrangements. But in the all-important human area of their own paternity, all male attempts at compensation fail, and the paternal role remains everywhere derivative, inferential, "uncertain, undefined, and perhaps unnecessary"! The basis is thus provided for the various cultural conditions of envy and imitation of woman's role and, correspondingly, for the appropriateness of the "womb-envying" concept.[11]

Shades of Freud and Adler! "Womb-envy" having been substituted for the well-known overly emphasized masculine envies and protests, and hurt "male vanity" for the much advertised vanity of women, the ground is perhaps finally cleared, in this supposed scientific age, for a more balanced and more objective consideration of this whole emotionally charged subject.

As Rank and others have maintained, it is an interesting subject for the cultural study of our time, that such a strange and unattractive theory as the Freudian, could obtain even the con-

---

10 *Ibid.,* pp. 288-89.

Not only is Freudian feminine psychology distorted, according to Rank, but, correspondingly, the psychology of the male, in which "the masculine qualities appear exaggerated to the point of caricature in a libidinal superman" . . . (*Beyond Psychology,* p. 287.) It is all part of Freud's "neurotic world-view" (*Ibid.,* p. 288) , in the service of which he interpreted the Greek Oedipus saga to fit his assumptions. "In his sensational interpretation," says Rank, "we find the social significance of a collective myth explained in terms of the highly individualized psychology of modern neurotics." (*Ibid.,* p. 122; Cf. Patrick Mullahy, *Oedipus, Myth and Complex,* chaps. VII, IX.)

11 *Male and Female,* chaps. IV, XVIII.

ditional acceptance which it has so long enjoyed among psycho-analysts, including women analysts. This could come about, according to him and other critics of the psychoanalytic view-point, only because Freud's position fitted in so well with our current prejudices as incorporated in our patriarchal culture, so that Freud's personal and decidedly biased views have been accepted uncritically as all-of-a-piece with the rest of his doctrine. But we are nevertheless dealing here, according to Rank, with a dramatic example of the cultural bias incorporated in the Freudian "masculinized" ideological system, an idea which Rank sought to suggest by entitling his special observations on the subject "Feminine Psychology and Masculine Ideology."

Rank's own more general views on the subject, while to some extent burdened with the biological orientation of his birth trauma theory and with a somewhat questionable conception of social evolution, nevertheless are also firmly anchored in his position on the relativity of psychological knowledge and the psychology of difference, in consequence of which he consistently maintained that in the complicated field of human behavior, we have *psychologies* and not a *psychology*. "As far as psychology is concerned, we have stated the problem," says Rank, "by claiming, besides a psychological difference of races, classes and individual types, an even more profound and universal difference in the psychology of man and woman." There is then, according to him, no more reason for describing the psychology of women negatively in terms of "lacks" on the basis of a comparison with the male than the other way around. On the biological level, according to him and in the view also of others, there is even less basis, inasmuch as there actually appears to be some ground for the notion of masculine biological "inferiority."[12]

But this whole approach in terms of "lacks" and "inferiorities" is suspect and objectionable from Rank's psychological

12 *Beyond Psychology*, pp. 251, 288.

standpoint, with his positive and constructive approach to psychological difference and his essentially democratic respect for personality. "Will people ever learn," he asks, "that there is no other equality possible than the equal right of every individual to become and to be himself, which actually means to accept his own difference and have it accepted by others?"[13] This is a question which he asks in this connection particularly, but with a suggestion of general applicability in relation to his conception of the need of a differential psychology of special psychological groups.

There are many interesting facets to Rank's views on this subject, since they are foundational in his theory and therapy, as already noted in various connections. But perhaps the most thought-provoking general aspect is the manner in which his feminine-centered perspective links up with his theory of creativity, especially creativity as it is related to the dramatic human events of pregnancy, birth, nursing and weaning, and child rearing. In all these respects, the male role is, of course, a negligible or, in any event, decidedly unspectacular one by comparison with the feminine role. The consequences of this situation upon the driving compulsive need of the male for substitute evidences of creative achievement which, in accordance with psychoanalytic doctrine, being substitute, are really never completely satisfying, provide a challenging and provocative new approach to the interpretation of many otherwise puzzling therapeutic as well as cultural phenomena. It is hardly surprising from this standpoint, for example, that both therapy and culture should disclose evidences of masculine envy of these dramatic feminine functions and prerogatives, just as Freud and Adler reported feminine envy of masculine functions and prerogatives.

"The woman creates biologically and really," says Rank, "while the man creates spiritually in unreality." This is a differ-

13 *Ibid.*, p. 267.

entiating life principle which expresses itself throughout the range of human activities, from the biological level to the ethical. "With the child as a creation," the woman has less need to create substitutively and to project, personify, and objectify culturally. "She can do it really in the child and eventually in the man," says Rank. He thus answers the question, so baffling to many, as to why women produce fewer works culturally: because, according to him, they create in reality and hence have less need to create in unreality![14] For the same reason, that is, that men do not bear and rarely nourish and rear children, nor cultivate their families and households, and increasingly under modern conditions of life, also the community welfare. Even Freud could hardly deny that this is creative work of the very highest human significance as well as social importance.

Once stated, the position appears so obvious as to seem self-evident. It is only ideological preconception that can obscure so fundamental a truth. "If poets and artists and philosophers," it has been said, "expended upon their works the love, thought, energy, and devotion that mothers commonly lavish upon their children, masterpieces—or at least near masterpieces—would not be as rare as they are!"

Rank's more detailed views, insofar as they have a bearing on the psychology of special groups, including the subject of feminine psychology, are bound up with the discussion of specific technical problems relating to therapy, philosophy, and art. They center about the conception that the mother-child relationship is primary and basic in human life and is the prototype of later anxiety, dependency, and developmental experiences for both men and women. This is a central theme which Rank developed in various directions, particularly in the discussion of therapeutic problems, and as such, has already been considered in previous connections. It is in the mother-child relationship, especially, that we grow into those human

14 *Will Therapy*, pp. 105-6; *Trauma of Birth*, p. 189; *Modern Education*, chap. I.

characteristics, traits, and values which distinguish human behavior and society. Perhaps it was because Freud so depreciated these human qualities that he also undervalued the maternal source of their development.

One further point is of interest in this connection. Art having been a focal interest with Rank throughout his career, he naturally made a most concentrated study of this area of investigation. He defines his approach most clearly, therefore, in relation to this subject-matter, in terms of a "social psychological probe" into the individual aspects of the subject and a "personal" approach to the collective ideological aspects. He says in this connection:

> "I propose to follow the line of reaching out beyond what is individual in the artist-personality and to show, or at least suggest, the collective aspect, whether as material, inspiration, or ultimate aim. My intention is to point out the relation between these two tendencies, inherent in art and in creativity: the individual and the collective, the personal and the social, in their interaction, and correspondingly in their counteraction."[15]

This may be taken as his considered formula for the correct approach to the interpretation of any complex human phenomenon, including feminine and masculine psychology. From this developed standpoint, it is at once evident how one-sided and inadequate was Freud's physiological approach and his supposition that feminine psychology is merely a special topic within the framework of a masculinized system of psychoanalytic doctrine, presented in generalized psychological terms.

Rank, like Jung and in contrast to Freud, introduced a positive approach to feminine psychology and, in this respect, he was certainly among the few outstanding pioneers who helped to bring about a more balanced outlook on the whole subject of feminine and masculine psychologies in modern analytic

---

[15] *Art and Artist*, pp. xiv, xxii.

theory. It is probably because Rank's views are imbedded in and get their chief meaning from technical subject-matter that his contributions in this area have not been more widely recognized. And if it be true, as some students think, that our present destructive culture is, in considerable measure, the product of a one-sided projection of masculine characteristics, with an overemphasis on aggressiveness, competitiveness, and the selfish aggrandizement of the market place and a corresponding under-valuation of the nourishing, cultivating, and humanizing qualities of the family circle, especially as represented by the mother-child relationship, then Rank's attempt to reorient analytic thought from a primary and focal concern with the masculine-centered Oedipus complex to the feminine-centered trauma of birth conception in its psychological, symbolic, and cultural implications, may not be the least of his many contributions to analytic as well as to more general thought.[16]

It is regrettable from this standpoint that discussion of Rank's birth trauma theory has centered so much around the controversial biological aspects of his original formulation that the wider and more important psychological and social aspects have been obscured. For it is these aspects which Rank stressed in his later formulations, in terms of the cultivation of human nature and social relations.

---

[16] The first effect of the birth trau.na theory was not so much to challenge the importance of the Oedipus complex as a principle of interpretation but to dethrone it from its position of primal importance, the latter being ascribed by Rank to the birth trauma, followed by weaning as a secondary trauma. Only after these two universally traumatic experiences, come the castration and Oedipus situations which, furthermore, according to Rank, take on force and meaning chiefly through a reactivation of the birth and weaning traumas. In his later thinking, however, Rank had less and less use for all these early principles of interpretation, his emphasis being directed increasingly to other theoretical concepts, particularly, as already noted, the concepts of will and relationship psychologically, socially, and culturally interpreted.

Chapter VIII

RECAPITULATION AND UNDERLYING PHILOSOPHY

"Our psychological age," by which he means the modern psychoanalytic age, according to Rank, was "inaugurated by Nietzsche and brought to a close by Freud, and can be best understood in its cultural significance if we apply the viewpoints and methods of both these men simultaneously to the comprehension of its development."[1] It is revealing to have the psychoanalytic movement linked up in this fashion with more general European thought which prepared the ground for the emergence of the psychoanalytic movement. In this larger setting, in which Rank likewise includes Schopenhauer and Ibsen as important figures, some of Freud's views appear less revolutionary than they were originally thought to be. It is seen, as Clara Thompson says, that "psychoanalysis did not spring full grown from the brow of Freud. It has a history."[2] And, it may be added, it also has more direct philosophic connections than was earlier recognized. For it has recently been established that Freud himself was better acquainted with European philosophical thought than was once supposed. In his later years, for

[1] *Beyond Psychology*, p. 271.
[2] Clara Thompson, *Psychoanalysis: Evolution and Development*, p. 3.

example, as a recent commentator notes, "Freud used to put a copy of Schopenhauer or Nietzsche in his pocket when he went on vacation."[3]

This larger cultural setting helps to explain especially Freud's negative approach to cultural values and why, as Rank says, "Freud's psychological system, which was supposed to be the result of scientific empiricism, has been received and taken up as an ideology fought for and against with a zeal only comparable to that shown in religious wars."[4] This orientation also links Rank up with the movement in a significant manner, his original identification with the same approach and his eventual departure from it.

In Rank's own background, Freud of course looms as the chief figure and Freudian thought as of primary and predominant importance, supplemented, however, as already noted, by special interests of his own and an intimate acquaintance with general psychological and philosophical thought. Particularly important in the latter connection, was the less direct and secondary influence of German voluntaristic thought, especially as represented by Schopenhauer's dynamic philosophy, which became an increasingly important factor in Rank's later work.

When Rank began to look about for a central concept around which to formulate the theoretical foundation of his deviating therapeutic procedure, he quite naturally turned to Schopenhauer's philosophy, in which he had long been interested and toward which many psychoanalysts were drawn, including Freud, by a feeling of kinship and basic dynamic conception. From Schopenhauer's philosophy, Rank took over the concept of "will," which he then redefined analytically and in terms of his own special therapeutic experiences, in such a way as to make his interpretations distinctively his own. It thus came

[3] Patrick Mullahy, Oedipus: Myth and Complex, p. 531; Siegfried Bernfeld, "Sigmund Freud, M.D., 1821-1885," International Journal of Psycho-analysis, Vol. XXXII (1951), pp. 204-17.
[4] Beyond Psychology, p. 272.

about that Rank undertook the later formulation of his therapeutic experiences in terms of will psychology and that his
therapy came to be known as "will therapy," through the appearance of the English translation of his *Technik der Psychoanalyse* (1926, 1929, 1931.) under the title *Will Therapy: An
Analysis of the Therapeutic Process in Terms of Relationship*
(1936). On the other hand, the concept of "relationship," which
is the core concept in his therapy just as his concept of "will"
is central in his psychology, as has already been observed, stems
more directly from his own therapeutic experience and his
trauma of birth theory, although the germ of the idea of birth
and rebirth likewise appears in Schopenhauer's voluntaristic
philosophy. But the special importance and significance which
these terms assumed in the later formulation of Rank's psychotherapy is an indication of the distinctive content which these
general concepts took on in the therapeutic framework of his
formulations.

It is also interesting to note, in view of the prominence which
some of these concepts have attained in modern social psychology and Rank's own increasing interest in this field, that the
following additional concepts are likewise featured in Rank's
later formulations: "situation," "process" and "role" which are
all considered in terms of therapy, and "personality" (development and types), "the social self," "individuation," "collective
ideology," and "social change," considered by extension more
generally and theoretically.

Commenting on the shift of outlook represented by these
new conceptions, Rank stated that they present a view of psychic
life which he to some extent anticipated even in his early work
Der Künstler (1905). However, he was able to develop the new
viewpoint only gradually on the basis of his analytic experience
and finally it crystallized into his will psychology, as outlined
in its practical aspects in his *Will Therapy* and in its theoretical
aspects in his *Truth and Reality*. Commenting further on the
matter, he observes:

"While I first was completely under the influence of Freudian realism, and tried to express my conception of the creative man, the artist, in biological-mechanistic terms of Freud's natural science ideology, on the basis of my own experience, I have since been enabled to formulate these common human problems in a common human language as well."[5]

The Trauma of Birth (1923), he notes, marked the decisive turning point in this development. There, he explains, he presented the creative drive as a "rebirth experience," understood psychologically "as the actual creative act of the human being." For in this act, "the psychic ego is born out of the biological corporeal ego and the human being becomes at once creator and creature or actually moves from creature to creator, in the ideal case, creator of himself, his own personality."

This conception of the relation of the creative act to the development of personality led him to another kind of treatment and presentation which set for itself the goal of viewing the two worlds, the individual and the broadly cultural as parallel. He describes the viewpoint further as follows:

"This involves not only the duality of actor and self-observor, but has yet another meaning, in that, for civilized man, the milieu is no longer the natural reality, the opposing force of the external world, but an artistic reality, created by himself which we, in its outer as in its inner aspects, designate a civilization. In this sense, civilized man, even if he fights the outside world, is no longer opposed to a natural enemy but at bottom to himself, to his own creation, as he finds himself mirrored, particularly in manners and customs, morality and conventions, social and cultural institutions. The phenomenon thus described is of fundamental meaning for the understanding of the human being's relation to the outer world as well as to his fellow man."[6]

[5] *Truth and Reality*, p. 4.
[6] *Ibid.*, pp. 6-7.

Against Freud's reality psychology and biological principle, he opposed "the spiritual principle which alone is meaningful in the development of the essentially human."

"This [principle] is based essentially on the conception that the inner world, taken in from the outside by means of identification has become in the course of time an independent power, which in its turn by way of projection, so influences and seeks to alter the external, that its correspondence to the inner is even more close. This relation to outer reality I designate as creation in contrast to adaptation, and comprehend as will phenomena. . . . . This conception of the influencing and transforming of the milieu by the individual allows for the inclusion of the creative, the artist type, for whom there is no place in Freud's world picture."[7]

The essential point in the creative process, according to him, is that the creative type "evolves his ego ideal from himself, not merely on the ground of given but also of self-chosen factors which he strives after consciously." In consequence, the ego, "instead of being caught between two powerful forces of fate, the inner id and the externally derived super-ego, develops and expresses itself creatively." The Freudian ego, Rank explains, becomes "almost a nonentity, a helpless tool for which there remains no autonomous function." Contrasting his own view, he says:

"In my view the ego is much more than a mere show place for the standing conflict between two great forces. Not only is the individual ego naturally the carrier of higher goals . . . it is also the temporal representative of the cosmic primal force no matter whether one calls it sexuality, libido, or id. The ego accordingly is strong just in the degree to which it *is* the representative of this primal force and the strength of this force represented in the individual we call the will."[8]

[7] *Ibid.*, pp. 7-8; *Art and Artist*, pp. 25-6.
[8] *Truth and Reality*, pp. 9-10.

These excerpts are cited to document several important aspects of Rank's changed orientation and perspective.

(1) In the first place, it is clear that Rank's will psychology is, as in the case of Adler's individual psychology, essentially an ego psychology, the ego or self or personality dominating the id, rather than the other way, as in the case of Freud. The psychological understanding of the creative type and its miscarriage in the neurotic, according to Rank, teaches us the value of the ego, not only as a wrestling ground of id impulses and super-ego repressions, "but also as conscious bearer of a striving force, that is, as the autonomous representative of the will and ethical obligation in terms of a self constituted ideal."

Rank's ego is thus not an entity merely mediating the conflicts of the impulsive life on the one hand and the restraining social world on the other. It is rather viewed as an inner-outer interdependent psycho-cultural unity, dynamically inter-related with its biological substratum and its socio-cultural milieu, and yet, at the same time, an effective influencing and transforming factor in itself, as expressed in the world of creative, ethical, and self-determining conduct.

(2) In the second place, it is evident that the problems of art, culture, and creativity in general were central in making Rank increasingly dissatisfied with the psychoanalytic conception of these phenomena. Not unlike the similar situation which had previously set Jung apart from Freud, the objection was to the negative interpretation of these phenomena which dominated psychoanalytic thought.

Like Jung, Rank gradually came to feel that the negative psychoanalytic view of culture and creativity in terms of the concept of sublimation was both "insipid and impotent" and did not even begin to approach the real psychological problems involved. Based as this view was, according to him, on an "overvaluation of the power of the unconscious impulsive life in man" and an "undervaluation of the conscious willing ego," the psychoanalytic interpretation treats these phenomena and ego psychology generally, "like a step-child" whereas, from his standpoint, "the conscious ego, with its willing, its sense of duty, and its feeling," and as bearer of the creative will, is at the very core of the creative and psychological process.

Psychoanalysis, according to Rank's view, incorporates a deep-seated contradiction between theory and practice in that its theory belittles the conscious ego while its practice represents "a glorification of the power of consciousness" in its emphasis on the therapeutic effectiveness of "making conscious the unconscious." This inconsistency, in his view, it can overcome only by a thoroughgoing revision of its ego psychology and its conception of the relation of id, ego, and super-ego in their respective effect on human behavior, rather than by the sort of patchwork revision of its underlying theory which characterized the later period of psychoanalytic development. Rank felt there has gradually been built up "a kind of psychic compulsion" toward this underlying theory, despite all evidence to the contrary.

(3) It is pertinent to inquire, in this connection, why Rank adopted the currently unpopular will concept, which he recognized had been discredited by "the old academic psychology," as the central concept of his reformulated psychology. It was precisely, he tells us, because this concept, redefined in analytic terms, tended to restore the factors neglected or undervalued by psychoanalytic theory that it particularly recommended itself to him. Among these factors, he noted specifically, as indicated above, the conscious ego and personality, the creative process, and the ethical sense of duty. In other connections, Rank also mentioned autonomy and the ability to choose, responsibility, and conscience.[9]

If we once acknowledge the power of the conscious ego, there appear interesting perspectives, according to him, "which the

[9] Freudian psychology, according to Rank, reduces man to a puppet and deprives personality of the very qualities, noted above, which make man's life human. (*Beyond Psychology*, p. 34.)

old academic psychology, in spite of its recognition of the meaning of conscious willing, could not let itself dream of because it lacked the dynamic viewpoint," presented by psychoanalysis in terms of biological instinct and by him in terms of creativity. "In a word," he declares, "we encounter here for the first time the actual ground of psychology," the realm of willing and ethics in psychic terms, the sphere of affect and human emotion as contrasted with instinct and hence slighted by psychoanalysis, the developing scope of human consciousness and self-consciousness. He explains:

> "The individual ego frees itself therefore always more and more with the weapon of increased power of consciousness, not only from the rule of environmental natural forces, but also from the biological reproduction compulsion of the overcome id; it influences thereby also more and more positively the super-ego development in terms of the self-constructed ideal formation and finally in a creative sense the outer world, whose transformation through men on its side again reacts upon the ego and its inner development.[10]

(4) Rank develops, in conjunction with this argument, his theory of psychological relativity, which runs through his reformulated will psychology. We are finally led back, according to him, from the problem of will to the problem of consciousness. For however fundamental and important the will "for all stimulation of the individual to acting, feeling and thinking, finally we can only comprehend all these phenomena in and through consciousness." And since consciousness itself and human knowledge as the expression of consciousness, are not fixed but relative developments, we are faced here with "a series of difficulties without knowledge of which every psychology is impossible, since the understanding of these contradictions forms the very warp and woof of psychology as such." We can

10 *Truth and Reality*, p. 18.

hardly do justice to this highly complicated state of affairs, he held, when we say that a constant interpretation and reinterpretation takes place from both sides—will and consciousness. This basic and interdependent process is obstructed by all one-sided and authoritarian doctrine, "for the essence of psychic processes consists in change and in the variability of the possibilities of interpretation."

Is there perhaps some way out of this flux of psychic events? asks Rank. His reply is as follows: "Certainly it is not the way of historical or genetic analysis" characteristic of psychoanalysis, for even the final elements to which we can arrive by this path still represents phenomena of interpretation, according to him. "There remains therewith psychologically no other recourse than just the recognition of this condition and perhaps also an attempt to understand why this is so," he asserts. And then, there is only the recurrent resort to and verification by direct experience, which remains the fountain-head and constantly renewable source of all psychological knowledge.[11]

The whole effect of Rank's complicated argument in this connection, is to point out that Freudian psychology is in these respects naive, over-simplified, and misleading to the point of actually being "anti-psychological," the psychoanalytic system, according to him, resting on preconceptions which are essentially divorced from genuine psychological considerations.

(5) It would seem from all this that Rank had traveled very far afield theoretically from his original Freudian background. In fact, Rank seems to have passed increasingly to the opposite theoretical pole, with his relativistic, voluntaristic, and humanistic outlook in contrast to the Freudian deterministic, mechanistic, and materialistic orientation. And yet concretely, this extreme theoretical contrast shades off essentially into a matter of relative importance and emphasis in regard to the specific issues and problems with which Rank was primarily concerned.

11 *Ibid.*, pp. 19-22.

For example, Rank emphasized "relationship" rather than "interpretation" in therapy, a contrast which is repeated in several of his well-known dualisms, such as, "knowing and experiencing," "past and present," "ideological and dynamic therapy," "truth and reality." But it is necessary to bear in mind that these contrasts are projected on the background of Freudian thought and procedure as a corrective of the constantly increasing emphasis on the theoretical structure of psychoanalysis. Furthermore, despite his criticism of the latter, Rank soon felt the need to formulate his own theory as a rationale and justification of his therapeutic innovations. What his contrasting emphasis on "relationship" as against "interpretation" amounts to concretely, therefore, is not that theory and interpretation are unimportant, but that they must not be fixed and unyielding to new experience and changing conditions. They must not, that is, be used "as a hampering curtain" between patient and therapist, but flexibly, open-mindedly, and above all, in the spirit of Rank's emphasis, creatively, an emphasis which naturally follows from his view of creativity in therapy and in personal development.

It is, therefore, not as if Rankians never use interpretation or Freudians concern themselves with relationship. It is rather a question of their relative importance and what use is made of them in the whole context of the therapeutic process which, in turn, is a matter of general frame of reference rather than of any specific technical device or contrast. It is on this account, that Rank always objected to the adoption of some specific technical device of his, such as the "time limit," and the attempt to incorporate it in an inconsistent framework of doctrine.

(6) It is accordingly necessary to inquire further into the significance of the change of theoretical outlook which Rank gradually arrived at in his later thought, as indicated above. What does this change of orientation signify more specifically? Psychologically, it means that Rank increasingly leaned toward what in Germany is termed the "cultural" as against the "nat-

ural science" approach to psychology; therapeutically, it means that he increasingly tended to stress therapy as an art rather than a science. This is a difference of conception which runs through the recent history of psychology as well as general thought.

In place of "the-world-is-a-machine" idea which dominates Freudian thought, including his psychology, this conception introduces into psychology a *human* frame of reference rather than a mechanical or even a biological one. It has a positive attitude toward human values, including religion, ethics, art, and culture generally. In fact, it is culture oriented, in consequence of which it receives its cultural designation.[12] It tends to be integrative, constructive, and appreciative in its approach to cultural phenomena, in contrast to the other view which tends to be analytical, reductive, and depreciative. Historically, this approach has been associated with interesting methodological innovations, in which the concepts of "intuition," "empathy," and "understanding" figure prominently. These concepts are not as familiar as the natural science concepts associated with the other approach, which have been popularized through three centuries of development, but they engage the subtleties and positive aspects of human interrelationship and culture in a manner altogether lacking in the other approach.

Just how these two approaches may be harmonized remains unsettled, but there is little question that both have a contribu-

12 Guilt as a psychological phenomenon is a good illustration of this difference of viewpoint. Commenting on the Freudian conception of guilt, Rank exclaims: "How presumptuous, and at the same time, naive, is this idea of simply removing human guilt by explaining it causally as 'neurotic'!" Brought up in the scientific ideology of the last century, Freud, according to Rank, used an approach meant to explain human behavior reductively, that is, from the most primitive biological plan which science has revealed as the basis of all life. But the whole history of mankind, according to him, "shows that human life is characterized by a denial of that very foundation," through a belief in spiritual immortality as against sexual mortality. By approaching the problem culturally, one can see clearly the moral conflict involved as the problem of problems in human psychology and "the deep need in the human being for just this kind of morality." (*Beyond Psychology*, pp. 273-74.)

tion to make to the interpretation and illumination of the complexities of human life. That this is an important consideration is becoming daily more apparent as we view the destruction which an extreme type of one-sided materialism has recently wrought in human affairs.

Even though the two conceptions appear, for the time being, to be in conflict theoretically, in practice, as noted, all sorts of compromises are possible. In Rank's case, furthermore, the contrast is considerably moderated by his procedure in presenting his position in relation to Freudian thought. This leads to a consideration of that "dynamic dualism," which Rank so frequently invoked in an effort to dramatize the polar contrasts precipitated by his later views when projected upon his earlier Freudian background.[13]

(7) Believing increasingly in the relativity of psychological theory and, in any event, in the still controversial character of psychological knowledge, Rank's characteristic method of presenting his later views was to project his new position upon the background of Freudian doctrine and by contrast, opposition, or affirmation to establish his particular view at the time. In this way, he felt, he was presenting both sides of the issues with which he was concerned and thus was avoiding the one-sided dogmatic presentation characteristic of Freudian doctrine. The method, termed by him "dynamic dualism," since it was Freudian doctrine primarily against which he was balancing his own views, has the disadvantage of seeming to deal in extremes, but the result of his presentation is to leave the door open to further and continued readjustment of views and evidence. This, in

[13] Dynamic dualism was for Rank a fundamental principle of life, manifest in all sorts of contrasts: male and female, heredity and environment, individual and collective, impulse and inhibition, positive and negative, etc. It represents one more adaptation of the Hegelian formula of thesis and antithesis. We are concerned here only with its consideration on the level of psychological theory in connection with which Rank says: "We must have something in contrast to which or against which we think," and in his case it was predominantly Freudian doctrine in contrast to which or against which he presented his own views. (*Will Therapy*, p. 65; *Beyond Psychology*, p. 22.)

fact, is the real significance and moderating import of his method, for Rank's dynamic dualism is not a fixed and static and dogmatic once-for-all solution; it is rather a dynamic and continuous process of resolution. It accounts for the differences of interpretation of Rank's position and the tolerant and constructive spirit in which he accepted these interpretations.[14]

Despite its concentration upon and even exaggeration of differences, the method accordingly points to open-mindedness in the consideration of one view against another, hence to flexibility and, in the spirit of Rank's theory, to creative choice in thought and procedure. This was certainly a necessary and important corrective historically and it remains a significant viewpoint today, although we can more accurately describe the present complex theoretical situation in terms of a dynamic "pluralism" rather than a "dualism." It is in this respect, nevertheless, that the following previously cited quotation from Kant which Rank features in his *Will Therapy,* so aptly characterizes the spirit of Rank's presentation: "You will learn from me not philosophy but to philosophize, not thoughts to be imitated but to think."

It should also be noted, however, that Rank's very method of presenting his position has kept his views close to Freudian

---

[14] Not claiming "scientific" validity for his views, Rank could tolerate differences of procedure and interpretation and utilize them for the advancement of his own position. Furthermore, he expected such differences because of his belief in the relativity of psychological theory. This tolerant attitude created a totally different atmosphere by comparison to the rigidities of psychoanalytic doctrine and technique. For example, in tracing out the background of his will psychology in terms of the related views of Schopenhauer, Nietzsche, and Freud, he says: "I do not doubt that my will psychology which has arisen from personal experiences, represents in its turn a reaction against Freud's 'making evil' of the will." (*Truth and Reality,* p. 37.) His will psychology, as he tells us further, "resulted not wholly from analytic experience, but also represents the result of my philosophic, pedagogic, religious and cultural studies." It was however, according to him, analytic practice that crystallized all these materials for him into a usable experience, and especially his own personal struggle in arriving at his distinctive conception of the analytic process. Recognizing, in this way, the cultural and personal aspects of his own views, he considered it inevitable that his views, in turn, should result in reinterpretations expressive of other conditions and backgrounds. (*Ibid.,* pp. 39-40.)

thought, even when he most definitely opposes the Freudian standpoint. For quite apart from the fact that Rank was not a systematic writer, so that he depended on the Freudian structure to provide a framework for his views, his method of polar presentation, in itself, kept his views closely interlinked with Freudian thought.

Jung and Adler set up systems of their own and thereby dissociated their positions almost completely from Freudian thought. Rank, on the other hand, never sought to detach himself completely from his Freudian background and, on this account, he did not feel the need to create a new system, a task toward which he was, in any event, temperamentally disinclined. He rather sought to build on the Freudian foundation and to support, supplement, revise, and eventually to attempt to correct it. Despite the opposition of some of his later views and of the increasingly distinctive setting of his own later theory, Rank accordingly remained all along closely identified with Freudian thought and issues. This helps to explain the more direct and continuing impact of his views on analytic thought and procedure, as well as on recent more general therapeutic developments.

(8) Rank's posthumously published volume, *Beyond Psychology* (1941), reflects a more extreme position in regard to some of the fundamental question considered here, for example, his views on the nature of psychological truth, the relation of the rational and the "irrational" in human life, and the role of collective ideologies in human behavior. But since Rank did not live to complete this volume, nor to see it in perspective so as to put it into final form, it is questionable whether these views should be permitted to distort his more carefully formulated position, as developed through the years since his separation from the Vienna group.

It is necessary to bear in mind that this final volume was prepared under the stress of a fatal illness and the disillusioning spectacle—so painful to Rank, as well as to many other cultured

Rank preceeding his death in 1939.

and sensitive Europeans, including Freud—of European culture seemingly engulfed in self-destruction. The work bears the scars of these painful experiences in the uncharacteristic pessimism and even fatalism which are reflected in such statements as the following: "There is a limit to all his [man's] efforts to control as long as death awaits the presumptuous conqueror of nature." And again: "We are born in pain, we die in pain, and we should accept life-pain as unavoidable."[15]

Having, however, noted these very understandable human aspects of the situation, this survey is nevertheless brought to a close with a reemphasis of Rank's position as outlined. For it is this position with which Rank has for years been identified and continues to be identified today.

In any event, no one is bound to accept Rank as a whole, not even his interpreters, as his dynamic dualism and his authorization of different points of emphasis demonstrate. You are invited to accept what you can use, provided it is accepted in the spirit of his basic pattern of thought, and to leave the rest to the test of time and further experience. This is in the best tradition of critical thought as well as scientific advance, despite the fact that Rank increasingly associated his position with philosophy rather than the type of science which he identified with Freudian doctrine. It was a principle which Rank endorsed with respect to all theoretical formulation, including his own.

The attempt throughout in this survey has been to stress those aspects of Rank's theory and therapy which have had a definite continuity in his work and writings, since, in the course of his development and in view of his deeply ingrained Freudian background, he necessarily held views which he later modified or discarded. The same principle is applied at this point. Rank introduced ideas in this final volume which, in some respects, seem to be inconsistent with his previously emphasized

15 *Beyond Psychology*, pp. 15-16.

views. This is simply noted without altering the basic pattern of the presentation.

(9) Where do all these lines of deviation leave Rank in relation to Freud? This must remain an open question to be determined by further developments, critical investigation, and therapeutic experience, in sifting out what is valid in each position. But meanwhile, Rank felt that his will therapy, emphasizing as it does, the strengthening of the personality in the direction of self-reliance, self-responsibility, and self-realization through creativity is the kind of therapeutic viewpoint which our modern complex, changing, and especially democratic society requires. An increasing number of his American adherents have tended to agree with him in this. And beyond the therapeutic consideration merely, there are broader social aspects which have had an extended appeal in a variety of therapy-related connections, as has already been noted. Altogether, it would seem, therefore, that Rank's position is headed for an important role in the further development of American psychotherapy and allied areas of endeavor.

MAJOR WORKS OF OTTO RANK (1884 - 1939)

In the order of their publication; only first editions and English translations are noted.

1. *Der Künstler,* 1907.
2. *Der Mythus der Geburt des Heldens,* 1909. Eng. trans. *The Myth of the Birth of the Hero,* 1914.
3. Ein Traum der Selbst deutet, *Jahrbuch für Psychoan.* II, 1910; *Psychoan. Rev.* V, 1918.
4. *Die Lohengrinsage,* 1911.
5. *Das Inzestmotiv in Dichtung und Sage,* 1912.
6. *Die Bedeutung der Psychoanalyse für die Geisteswissenschaften* (with H. Sachs), 1913. Eng. trans. *The Significance of Psychoanalysis for the Mental Sciences,* 1916.
7. Homer: Psychologische Beiträge zur Entstehungsgeschichte des Volksepos, *Imago* V, 1917.
8. Das Volksepos: Die dichterische Phantasiebildung, *Imago* V, 1917.
9. *Psychoanalytische Beiträge zur Mythenforschung,* 1919.
10. *Die Don Juan Gestalt,* 1924. (*Imago* VIII, 1922; *Psychoan. Rev.* XIII, 1926.)
11. *Eine Neurosenanalyse in Träumen,* 1924.
12. Der Doppelgänger, 1925. (*Imago* III, 1914; *Psychoan. Rev.* VI, 1919.)
13. *Entwicklungsziele der Psychoanalyse* (with S. Ferenczi), 1924. Eng. trans. *The Development of Psychoanalysis,* 1925.
14. *Sexualität und Schuldgefühl,* 1926, (*Internat'l Jour. of Psychoan.* IV, 1923.)
15. *Das Trauma der Geburt,* 1924. Eng. trans. *The Trauma of Birth,* 1929.
16. *Technik der Psychoanalyse.*
    Vol. I, *Die analytische Situation,* 1926.
    Vol. II, *Die analytische Reaktion,* 1929.
    Vol. III, *Die Analyse des Analytikers,* 1931.
    Eng. trans. of volumes II and III together with a summary of volume I, *Will Therapy,* 1936.

17. *Grundzüge einer genetischen Psychologie auf Grund der Psychoanalyse der Ich-Struktur.*
   Vol. I, *Genetische Psychologie,* 1927.
   Vol. II, *Gestaltung und Ausdruck der Persönlichkeit,* 1928. *(Psychoan. Rev.* XVI, 1929.)
   Vol. III, *Wahrheit und Wirklichkeit,* 1929. Eng. trans. *Truth and Reality,* 1936.

18. *Seelenglaube und Psychologie,* 1931. Eng. trans. *Psychology and the Soul,* 1950.

19. *Modern Education,* 1932.

20. *Art and Artist,* 1932.

21. *Beyond Psychology,* 1941. (Posthumously published by friends and students.)

REFERENCES

Adler, Alfred, *A Study of Organ Inferiority and Its Psychical Compensation* (translated by S. E. Jeliffe), Nervous and Mental Disease Publishing Co., New York, 1917.

————, *The Neurotic Constitution* (translated by B. Glueck and J. E. Lind), Moffat, Yard & Co., New York, 1917.

————, *The Practice and Theory of Individual Psychology* (translated by P. Radin), Harcourt, Brace & Co., New York, 1924.

————, *Understanding Human Nature*, (translated by W. Béran Wolfe), Greenberg, New York, 1927.

————, "Individual Psychology" in Carl Murchison (ed.), *Psychologies of 1930*, Clark University Press, Worcester, Mass., 1930.

————, *Social Interest: A Challenge to Mankind* (translated by J. Linton and R. Vaughan), Faber and Faber, London, 1938.

Alexander, Franz and French, Thomas M., *Psychoanalytic Therapy: Principles and Application*, Ronald Press Co., New York, 1946.

Allen, Frederick H. *Psychotherapy with Children*, W. W. Norton & Co., New York, 1942.

Aptekar, Herbert H., *Basic Concepts in Social Case Work*, University of North Carolina Press, Chapel Hill, 1941.

Bailey, Pearce, "An Introduction to Rankian Psychology," *Psychoanalytic Review*, Vol. XXII (1935) pp. 182-211.

Benedict, Ruth F., *Patterns of Culture*, Houghton Mifflin Co., Boston, 1934.

Bernard, L. L., *Instinct: A Study in Social Psychology*, Henry Holt & Co., New York, 1924.

Boas, Franz, *Anthropology and Modern Life*, W. W. Norton & Co., New York, 1928.

A. A. Brill (trans. and ed.) *The Basic Writings of Sigmund Freud*, Modern Library, Random House, New York, 1938.

Cantor, Nathaniel, *The Dynamics of Learning*, Foster and Stewart Publ. Corp., Buffalo, N. Y., 1946.

————, *Learning Through Discussion*, Human Relations for Industry, Buffalo, N. Y., 1951.

Cassirer, Ernst, *Essay on Man*, Yale University Press, New Haven, Conn., 1944.

Deutsch, Helene, *Psychology of Women*, Grune & Stratton, New York, 1944-45.

Faris, Ellsworth, *The Nature of Human Nature*, McGraw-Hill Book Co., New York, 1937.

117

Fenichel, Otto, *The Psychoanalytic Theory of Neurosis*, W. W. Norton & Co., New York, 1945.

Freud, Sigmund, *A General Introduction to Psychoanalysis* (translated by G. S. Hall), H. Liveright, New York, 1920.

————, *New Introductory Lectures on Psychoanalysis* (translated by W. J. H. Sprott), W. W. Norton & Co., New York, 1933.

————, *Three Contributions to the Theory of Sex* (translated by A. A. Brill), Nervous and Mental Disease Publishing Co., New York, 1916.

————, *The Ego and the Id* (translated by Joan Riviere), Hogarth Press, London, 1927.

————, *Beyond the Pleasure Principle* (translated by C. J. M. Hubback), Boni & Liveright, New York, 1924.

————, *Collected Papers* (translated by Joan Riviere and others), Hogarth Press, London, 1924-25.

————, *The Problem of Anxiety* (translated by H. A. Bunker), W. W. Norton' & Co., New York, 1936.

————, *Civilization and Its Discontents* (translated by Joan Riviere), Hogarth Press, London, 1939.

Fromm Erich, *Escape From Freedom*, Farrar & Rinehart, New York, 1941.

Gomberg, R. M. and Levingson, F. T. (ed.), *Diagnosis and Process in Family Counseling*, Family Service Association of American, New York, 1951.

Healy, W., Bronner, A. F. and Bowers, A. M., *The Structure and Meaning of Psychoanalysis*, Alfred A. Knopf, New York, 1931.

Hendrick, Ives, *Facts and Theories of Psychoanalysis*, Alfred A. Knopf, New York, 1934.

Hollis, E. V. and Taylor, A. L., *Social Work Education in the United States*, Columbia University Press, New York, 1951.

Horney, Karen, *The Neurotic Personality of Our Time*, W. W. Norton & Co., New York, 1937.

————, *New Ways in Psychoanalysis*, W. W. Norton & Co., New York, 1939.

James, William, *The Principles of Psychology*, Henry Holt & Co., New York, 1890.

Jung, C. G., *The Psychology of the Unconscious* (translated by B. M. Hinkle), Moffat, Yard & Co., New York, 1916.

————, *Psychological Types* (translated by H. G. Baynes), Harcourt, Brace & Co., New York, 1923.

————, *Collected Papers on Analytical Psychology* (translated by C. E. Long), Bailliere, Tindall & Cox, London, 1920.

————, *Contributions to Analytical Psychology* (translated by H. G. and C. F. Baynes), Harcourt, Brace & Co., New York, 1928.

————, *Modern Man in Search of a Soul* (translated by W. S. Dell and C. F. Baynes), Harcourt, Brace & Co., New York, 1934.

————, *The Integration of the Personality* (translated by G. M. Dell), Farrar & Rinehart, New York, 1939.

Kardiner, Abram, *The Individual and His Society,* Columbia University Press, New York, 1939.

Karpf, Fay B., *American Social Psychology, Its Origins, Development, and European Background,* McGraw-Hill Book Co., New York, 1932.

——, *Dynamic Relationships Therapy* (brochure), Social Work Technique, Los Angeles, 1937.

——, *Personality From the Standpoint of Rankian "Will" or "Dynamic Relationship" Psychology* (brochure), Social Work Technique, Los Angeles, 1940.

Kasius, Cora (ed.), *A Comparison of Diagnostic and Functional Casework Concepts,* Family Service Association of America, New York, 1950.

Klein, D. B., *Abnormal Psychology,* Henry Holt & Co., New York, 1951.

Kluckhohn, C. and Murray, H. A. (eds.), *Personality in Nature, Society and Culture,* Alfred A. Knopf, New York, 1948.

Kranefeldt, W. M., *Secret Ways of the Mind* (translated by R. M. Eaton), Henry Holt & Co., New York, 1932.

Linton, Ralph (ed.), *The Science of Man in the World Crisis,* Columbia University Press, New York, 1945.

May, Rollo, *The Meaning of Anxiety,* Ronald Press Co., New York, 1950.

McDougall, William, *Psychoanalysis and Social Psychology,* Methuen & Co., London, 1936.

Murphy, G., Jensen, F. and Levy, J., *Approaches to Personality,* Coward-McCann, New York, 1932.

——— G., *An Historical Introduction to Modern Psychology,* Harcourt, Brace & Co., New York, 1930.

Mead, Margaret, *Male and Female,* William Morrow & Co., New York, 1949.

Mullahy, Patrick, *Oedipus, Myth and Complex,* Hermitage Press, New York, 1948.

Plant, J. S., *Personality and the Cultural Pattern,* Commonwealth Fund, New York, 1937.

Parsons, Talcott, *The Social System,* Free Press, Glencoe, Ill., 1951.

Phillips, Helen U. (ed.), *Achievement of Responsible Behavior Through Group Work Process,* University of Pennsylvania Press, Philadelphia, 1950.

Rank, Otto (with S. Ferenczi), *The Development of Psychoanalysis* (translated by C. Newton), Nervous and Mental Disease Publishing Co., New York, 1925.

——, *The Trauma of Birth* (translated from the German), Harcourt, Brace & Co., New York, 1929.

——, *Art and Artist, Creative Urge and Personality Development* (translated by C. F. Atkinson), Alfred A. Knopf, New York, 1932.

——, *Modern Education, A Critique of Its Fundamental Ideas* (translated by M. E. Moxon), Alfred A. Knopf, New York, 1932.

119

————, *Will Therapy, An Analysis of the Therapeutic Process in Terms of Relationship* (translated by J. Taft), Alfred A. Knopf, New York, 1936.

————, *Truth and Reality, A Life History of the Human Will* (translated by J. Taft), Alfred A. Knopf, New York, 1936.

————, *Gundzüge einer genetischen Psychologie auf Grund der Psychoanalyse der Ichstruktur*, Vol. I, *Genetische Psychologie*, Franz Deuticke, Leipzig u. Wien, 1927. (Translated from the German in typescript); Vol. II, *Gestaltung und Ausdruck der Persönlichkeit*, Franz Deuticke, Leipzig u. Wien, 1928. (Translated from the German in typescript).

————, *Beyond Psychology*, Haddon Craftsmen, Camden, N. J., 1941.

Reik, Theodor, *From Thirty Years With Freud* (translated by R. Winston), International Universities Press, New York, 1949.

*Robinson, Virginia P., *A Changing Psychology in Social Case Work*, University of North Carolina Press, Chapel Hill, 1930.

————, *The Dynamics of Supervision Under Functional Control*, University of Pennsylvania Press, Philadelphia, 1949.

Rogers, Carl R., *Counseling and Psychotherapy*, Houghton Mifflin Co., Boston, 1942.

————, *Client-Centered Therapy*, Houghton Mifflin Co., Boston, 1951.

Ruesch, J. and Bateson, G., *Communication: The Social Matrix of Psychiatry*, W. W. Norton & Co., New York, 1951.

Sachs, Hanns, *Freud, Master and Friend*, Harvard University Press, Cambridge, Mass., 1944.

Sargent, S. S. and Smith, M. W. (eds.), *Culture and Personality*, Viking Fund, New York, 1949.

Sears, R. R., *Survey of Objective Studies of Psychoanalytic Concepts*, Social Science Research Council, New York, 1943.

*Taft, Jessie, *The Dynamics of Therapy in a Controlled Relationship*, Macmillan Co., New York, 1933.

———— (ed.), *Family Casework and Counseling: A Functional Approach*, University of Pennsylvania Press, Philadelphia, 1948.

Thomas, W. I., *Primitive Behavior: An Introduction to the Social Sciences*, McGraw-Hill Book Co., New York, 1937.

Thompson, Clara, *Psychoanalysis, Evolution and Development*, Hermitage House, New York, 1950.

Thorne, Frederick C., *Principles of Personality Counseling*, Journal of Clinical Psychology, Brandon, Vt., 1950.

Wittels, Fritz, *Freud and His Time* (translated by L. Brink), H. Liveright, New York, 1931.

* A series of publications by these authors is available, seeking to interpret Rank's views in their application to various areas and problems in the fields of therapy, counseling, education, and social work. A few illustrative references have been included in the bibliography to indicate the influence of these publications in these connections. See also note pp. 84-5.

Woodworth, R. S., *Contemporary Schools of Psychology*, Ronald Press Co., New York, 1931.

Zilboorg, Gregory, *A History of Medical Psychology*, W. W. Norton & Co., New York, 1941.

Ziskind, Eugene, *Psycho-Physiological Medicine for the General Practitioner* (To be published in 1953).

Znaniecki, Florian, *Cultural Sciences: Their Origin and Development*, University of Illinois Press, Urbana, 1952.

INDEX

Community work, vi
Comparative religion, 33
Compensation, 40-41, 98
Complex, castration, 43, 98
  inferiority, 40-1, 44, 92
  Oedipus, 51, 56, 58, 90, 98
conscience, 105
conscious (the), 34, 72, 104 ff.
consciousness, 25, 26, 69, 72, 105, 106, 107
Constructive approach (in therapy), 12, 35, 37, 45, 54, 58, 59, 61, 65
  to culture, 109
  to psychological difference, 95
  to reintegration, 35
Control, 53, 54, 55, 72
  limitations of, 113
Cooperation, social (see Social cooperation)
Creative, action, 53, 62, 102
  force, 42
  imagination, 38
  impulse, 71, 102
  principle, 33
  spirit, 36
  tendency, 37
  therapy, 108
  transformation of instinct, 72
  type (see Artistic or creative type)
  view, 81
  will, 69, 71
Creativity, 4, 53, 69, 78, 79, 95, 96, 97, 106, 108, 111, 114
  in contrast to adaptation, 103
  negative interpretation of, 104
Criminal type (see Anti-social type)
Counseling, vi, 16, 83-86
Culture, 13, 14, 33, 34, 52, 66, 104, 109
  history, 5
  negative approach to, 100, 104
  oriented approach, 92, 109
  patriarchal, 94
  and personality, v, 5
  and psychoanalysis (see Applied psychoanalysis)
Cultural, anthropology, 12, 38, 67, 93, 108
  change (see Social change)
  development, 33, 94
  dynamics, 5
  orientation and perspective, 5, 92, 108-109

science, 12

Death instinct, 23, 54
Denial, 51, 70, 109
  of responsibility, 72
  of willing, 70, 72
Dependency, 40, 58, 96
  mother-centered conception, 58
Depth psychology, 36, 45, 90
Der Künstler (The Artist), 3, 65, 70, 101
Determinism, psychic, 54, 55, 81, 107
Deutsch, Helene, 92
The Development of Psychoanalysis, 7, 50
Dialectic of human growth and development, 75, 79
Difference, psychology of, 16, 94, 95, 111
Direct experience, importance of in Rankian theory, 107
Dream analysis, 23, 33, 44, 55 ff.
Disorientation, 35
Disorganization, 35
Dualism, dynamic, 102, 108, 110-112, 113
Dynamic relationship psychology (see Will psychology)
Dynamic relationship therapy (see Will therapy)
Dynamics, cultural, 5
  group, 12
  in therapy, 52, 57, 58, 59

Education, vi, 12, 16, 17, 37, 44, 61, 83
Ego, in psychoanalysis, 23, 39, 41, 43, 69,
  (self) psychology, 39, 60, 69, 72, 102-106 (see also Self and Personality)
  ego-ideal, 69, 103, 106
Eitingon, Max, iii
Elan vital, 32
Ellis, Havelock, v
Emotion, 69, 106
Emotional, release, 34
  dynamics, importance of, 56
Empathy, 109
Ending, in therapy, 57, 58, 59, 91
Eros, 23
Ethics, 38, 104, 105, 106, 109

ADDENDUM TO THE 1970 REPRINT EDITION

With this reprinting, the question naturally presented itself as to whether the book should be retained in its original form or an attempt be made at updating especially the bibliographical referencing. Technical and historical considerations finally decided in favor of the first alternative, thus retaining the book as an historical record. At the same time,this reprinting suggests the continued relevance of many of Rank's views to a variety of recent developments in psychotherapy, among them "short" therapy, time-limited therapy, client-centered and non-directive therapy, art and creativity in therapy, even humanism and existentialism, and now also the renewed emphasis on "will," which has been used for decades as a distinctive characterization of Rankian psychotherapy in connection with other schools of psychoanalysis and psychotherapy.

With all this in view, the following items are added to fill out the foregoing account by prominent representation of the more recent literature dealing with important aspects of Rank's life, work, theory and therapy from various standpoints.

Alexander, F., Eisenstein, S. and Grotjahn, M. (eds.), *Psychoanalytic Pioneers*, Basic Books, New York, 1966.

Alexander, F. G. and Selesnick, S. T., *The History of Psychiatry*, Harper and Row, Inc., New York, 1966.

Allport, Gordon W., *Personality and Social Encounter*, Beacon Press, Boston, 1960.

Faatz, Anita J., *The Nature of Choice in Casework Process,* University of North Carolina Press, Chapel Hill, 1953.

Farber, Leslie H., *The Ways of the Will*, Basic Books, Inc., 1966.

Ford, Donald H. and Urban, Hugh B., *Systems of Psychotherapy*, John Wiley and Sons, Inc., New York, 1963.

Hall, Calvin S. and Lindsey, Gardner, *Theories of Personality*, John Wiley and Sons, Inc., New York, 1957.

Jones, Ernest, *The Life and Work of Sigmund Freud*, Basic Books, New York, 1957.

Karpf, Fay B., "Rankian Will or Dynamic Relationship Therapy," *Progress in Psychotherapy*, Vol. II (1957) Masserman, J. H. and Moreno, J. L. (eds.), Grune and Stratton, New York, 1957.

May, Rollo, *Love and Will*, W. W. Norton & Co., Inc., New York, 1969.

Moustakas, Clark E., *Psychotherapy with Children*, Harper Brothers, New York, 1959.

Munroe, Ruth L., *Schools of Psychoanalytic Thought*, Dryden Press, Inc., New York, 1955.

Progoff, Ira, *The Death and Rebirth of Psychology*, Julian Press, Inc., New York, 1956.

Robinson, Virginia P. (ed.), *Jessie Taft*, University of Pennsylvania Press, Philadelphia, 1962.

Smalley, Ruth Elizabeth, *Theory for Social Work Practice*, Columbia University Press, New York, 1967.

Taft, Jessie, *Otto Rank*, Julian Press, Inc., New York, 1958.

Wolberg, Lewis R., *The Technique of Psychotherapy*, Grune and Stratton, New York, 1954.

Special attention is directed to the *Journal of the Otto Rank Association* which concerns itself primarily with Rank materials and with matters of Rankian interest; also to the Otto Rank Association, the purpose of which is "to foster and develop interest in the writings of Dr. Otto Rank (1884-1939)" and "to promote further exploration of his concepts and their meaning for art, literature, psychology, psychotherapy, and the history of culture."